WAR AT SEA

BLITZ EDITIONS

Published by Blitz Editions
an imprint of Bookmart Ltd
Registered Number 2372865
Trading as Bookmart Ltd
Desford Road
Enderby
Leicester LE9 5AD

ISBN 1 85605 265 6

This material has previously appeared in *Witness to World War II.*

PICTURE CREDITS
The publisher would like to thank the following organisations for supplying photographs for use in this book.
Every effort has been made to contact the copyright holders for the pictures. In some cases they have been untraceable, for which we offer our apologies.

US National Archives; VSEL Vickers; Imperial War Museum; Bundesarchiv; Bibliothek fur Zeitgeschichte; Ufficio Storico Fototeca; National Maritime Museum; J Baker Collection; USAF Photo; US Navy Photo Section; US Coast Guard; Australian High Commission, London.

THE AUTHOR
Karen Farrington is a writer and former Fleet Street journalist who has specialised in the study of conflict throughout the 20th Century. In compiling Witness to World War II she has personally interviewed scores of veterans from around the world, obtaining a unique insight into the war through the eyes of the men on the front line. Among her previous books is 'Fated Destiny', an historical pot pourri of the curious, shocking and mysterious which includes accounts of some of the greatest military blunders in recent history. Karen Farrington is married with three children and lives in Exmoor, Devon.

This book was produced by Amazon Publishing Limited
Designed by Wilson Design Associates

Printed in the Czech Republic
51762

War at Sea

WEAPONS AT SEA

For years naval warfare had remained largely unchanged. It was a case of tactics combining with firepower to achieve the victories sought after by the seafaring nations.

Britain excelled at the art of the sea battle and was proud of her navy traditions. By 1939, however, the rules of the game had changed and, unfortunately, nobody informed the major players.

No longer was it enough to have impressively large ships capable of blasting the enemy vessels out of the water. In fact, capital ships were a positive disadvantage as they were large targets which could only move slowly to evade enemy fire. It meant Germany's Bismarck and Tirpitz ships and Japan's Yamato were obsolete when they originally rolled down the slipway in time to see action during World War II. The great hopes that they carried with them were badly misplaced.

The power lay with aircraft and a navy was only as good as its fleet air arm. Britain didn't have a fleet air arm at all as it had been incorporated into the Royal Air Force. Many British naval chiefs refused to believe the age of the big ships had drawn to a close. It took the death of the battleship Prince of Wales and battle cruiser Repulse off the coast of Malaya in December 1941 at the hands of Japan's skilful fliers to convince them of the fact.

Now ships would stay out of reach of enemy guns and send in versatile and effective planes to wreak havoc with opposition navies. As the range of the aircraft increased through the war, the big ships could stay hundreds of miles away from the hub of the fighting.

The power lay with aircraft and a navy was only as good as its fleet air arm

Britain was, however, better placed regarding the advent of navy planes than Germany. At least the British could call on seven aircraft carriers, including the Ark Royal and Illustrious during the conflict. Hitler, in contrast, had only one aircraft carrier in his navy, Graf Zeppelin, which was never completed.

ARMOUR PLATING

The importance of air battles at sea in turn made the bodily defences of each ship key to its survival. Each navy discovered to its cost that only the thickest armour plating was impervious to bombs dropped by

Left: **Mangled wreckage after the surprise Japanese strike at Pearl Harbor, revealing the scale of damage inflicted.**
Below: Illustrious **was one of Britain's few aircraft carriers at the outbreak of war.**

planes. Those ships which crumpled easily under fire from above were the first casualties of the conflict.

At the start of the war, Britain had the largest navy in the world – 12 battleships, three battle cruisers, 15 heavy and 45 light cruisers, 184 destroyers, 58 submarines and 27 motor torpedo boats. The navy was probably in better shape than the army or the air force but still unprepared for war. At least there was a construction programme that would considerably improve the size of the navy. The largest British ship was Hood, sunk by Bismarck in 1941.

◆ EYE WITNESS ◆

George Miles enlisted in the Australian Army in 1940 when he was 17 years old. He was injured at El Duda in North Africa, and was being ferried to hospital in December 1941 when his ship was blown up in the Mediterranean.

❛There were about 600 people on the *Chaktina*, mostly wounded although there were some prisoners of war. Only 200 survived, including a German general. Out of 17 members of my battalion, I was among three who lived. We were headed for the 62nd General Hospital in Alexandria. It was night-time when the Italian dive-bombers struck. The sky lit up as if it was day. The ship was blown apart. In the melée you didn't get a chance to worry about anything.

I had a life jacket on. I spent time in a life raft or clinging to the side – it was so crowded that you had to take your turn.

We pushed dying men over the side to let the rest live. It was the following night when we were picked up by a Norwegian corvette.❜

Left: **Human torpedoes, nicknamed 'pigs', were launched from this tiny hatch on the Italian tanker *Olterra*.**

The largest of the British ships was* Hood, *sunk by* Bismarck *in 1941

Italy had a sizeable navy consisting of six modern battleships, 19 cruisers, 132 destroyers and torpedo boats and 107 submarines.

In Japan's navy when it entered the war in 1941 the number of aircraft carriers outnumbered the number of battleships by 11 to ten. This accounts for Japan's success on the high seas in the opening months of the war. Also lining up under the emblem of the rising sun were 23 cruisers, 129 destroyers, 67 submarines and 13 gunboats.

Much of the American strength in the area was decimated by the attack on Pearl Harbor. For months US shipyards laboured to repair the damage wrought by the Japanese planes and refloated many of the sunken vessels. America only had

On the other hand, the German navy was the least favoured branch of Hitler's armed forces. He promised his Admiral Erich Raeder plenty of time to prepare for war in Europe. The conflict arrived about five years too early, as far as Raeder was concerned.

He had two battleships, Scharnhorst and Gneisenau, in readiness as well as three pocket battleships. In addition there were seven cruisers, 21 destroyers and 12 torpedo boats in the fleet. His strengths lay in U-boats, of which he had 159 and planned many more. He also made good use of auxiliary cruisers or armed raiders, as they were better known. Merchant ships in their appearance and war ships in their weaponry, they launched bandit attacks on shipping throughout the world.

three operational aircraft carriers in the Pacific, 24 cruisers, nine battleships, 80 destroyers and 56 submarines. The hidden weapon that America possessed was its ability to produce sufficient replacements and reinforcements for its navy throughout the war.

Submarines also came of age during World War II, although only Germany and America fully grasped the potential offered by this sleek, sinister vessel.

The German U-boats could very well have changed the entire course of World War II if only there had been enough of them during the crucial early years. Hitler saw too late the massive opportunity he had passed up by reining in resources due to his navy.

American submarines executed a brilliant strategic move against Japan, destroying the vast majority of its merchant shipping and isolating the four home islands from outside trade, effectively starving the people and industry of vital goods. Any other country which did not have the shame and dishonour of surrender woven deeply into its culture would have surrendered on the strength of the submarine stranglehold alone.

The Allies possessed one ace which helped them considerably in their war at sea. It was radar or, to give it its proper name, radio detection and ranging. Pioneering scientist Sir Robert Watson-Watt developed the system during the twenties and thirties and personally oversaw its use for the benefit of all the British military following the outbreak of World War II.

Astonishing advances made in code-breaking offered plenty of new chances to the fleet

Radar detects distant objects by sending out a microwave pulse beam. The reflection of the beam indicates the position of the object.

Its advantage to the Allies at sea was soon apparent. They would get fair warning of approaching enemy ships and planes. Bad weather was no longer the cloak to vision it once had been. Action under cover of darkness would now achieve more accurate results.

CODE-BREAKING

Also at sea, the astonishing advances made in code-breaking offered many new chances to the fleet who were forewarned about enemy movements.

The Italians came up with some ingenious waterborne methods of attack. The first was an Explosive Motor Boat with a one-man crew. The bows of the boat were packed with explosives which would fire on impact. It wasn't a suicide vehicle. The courageous pilot escaped by throwing himself backwards with a float before the EMB made contact with its target.

Also among their gadgets was a torpedo submarine measuring about 22 ft which was driven by a two-man crew sitting astride the strange weapon. Cast into the water by full-sized submarines, the men wearing diving suits guided this timed missile towards its target and attached it to the underside of a ship's hull before making an escape.

Above: **It took courage and endurance to man the Italian torpedoes which wreaked havoc in the Mediterranean.**

The British, too, had their midget submarines. These were based on an early submarine design, it was 51ft long, eight and a half feet wide and ten feet high. Inside there was just enough space for four crew members, a commander, a lieutenant to operate the engine, a navigator and an engineer. The capabilities of the midget submarines were most impressive. They could dive to a depth of 300ft and boasted a speed of four knots.

GRAF SPEE

When war was declared, the British people expected an instant torrent of bombs to fall from a sky blackened by enemy aircraft. The wail of the air raid siren sent people scurrying for shelter clutching their gas masks in fear of being enveloped in a cloud of poisonous chemicals.

It didn't happen and soon the opening stages of the war were labelled 'the Phoney war' or even 'the Bore War'. The sceptics at home who believed the war would be over once Hitler had his way in Poland had to wait nearly a year to see action over Britain. But at sea it was an entirely different story.

A lone U-boat set the tenor of the sea-farers conflict when the liner Athenia sailing out of Glasgow was sunk off Ireland the day after hostilities were officially opened. U-boat captain Fritz-Julius Lemp believed he had an auxiliary cruiser or troopship in his sights. In all, 112 lives were lost including 28 Americans. There was shock at such an atrocity, even in Germany, and it prompted fresh orders to the U-boat commanders, to target only freighters and Navy ships. It was only a matter of months before the tighter rules which governed the U-boats were disregarded once more, however.

More than 800 sailors died when a U-boat slid into Scapa Flow and destroyed a battleship

The brutal attack on Athenia sparked an Allied blockade of Germany in which ships were stopped and searched at the rate of 100 a week. Although the Royal Navy did capture some German ships this way, it caused acrimony between Britain and other neutral countries who resented the intrusive action.

By the end of September 1939, 20 Allied ships had been floored by U-boats, including HMS Courageous, lost in the Atlantic with 515 men. Even neutral boats heading to Britain bearing vital supplies were not safe from the prowling German submarines. Already the spectre of life without the benefit of essential sea-borne trading links was looming in Britain.

MAGNETIC MINES

Britain's mariners fared little better in October. More than 800 sailors died when a U-boat slid into Scapa Flow, the anchorage of the British Fleet 10 miles off the north coast of Scotland, which was thought to be a safe haven, and destroyed a large British battleship. Under the command of Captain Gunther Prien, the submarine manoeuvred through a narrow, unguarded channel leading into the harbour area and dealt a deadly blow to the Royal Oak. Claims that the battleship's armour could withstand a torpedo attack proved to be nothing more than a pipe dream. Just 396 members of the 1200-strong crew survived.

Shipping not only had to contend with the phantom U-boats. Germany was laying hundreds of mines, with devastating effect. The Reich had pioneered a deadly magnetic mine which could be dropped by air on to the sea bed, to later rise and attach itself to any passing ship, with deadly consequences. It was far superior to the mines being laid by Britain, designed to defend its shipping.

Fortunately, one of the mystery mines was jettisoned in error on land. Thanks to one courageous naval officer who tackled the explosive, its secret of success became known. The antidote was 'de-gaussing', with an electric cable fitted to ships which neutralised magnetism. The plague of the magnetic mine at least to British ships was quickly overcome.

Above: **After the Battle of the River Plate the *Graf Spee* limped into Montevideo for repairs. However, it could not escape its predators for long.**

Left: **U-boat Captain Gunther Prien was hailed a hero in his homeland for penetrating Scapa Flow.**

Above the waves were the determined ships of the Reich's navy equally adept at picking off British vessels. Among them was the pocket battleship Admiral Graf Spee. By agreement before the war, the Germans were only supposed to build ships up to a certain size. These were tagged pocket battleships, larger than cruisers but smaller and less effective than battleships.

The Graf Spee slipped out of port just before war was declared, sidestepped the ensuing Royal Navy blockade and headed for the South Atlantic. It was then the pride of the German navy with its high speed and thick protective plating. In the first three months of the war, it had notched up nine British ships, including the liner, Doric Star.

Canny British commander Commodore H. Harwood guessed that it was only a matter of time before the Graf Spee was lured to the River Plate, Uruguay, attracted by the rich vein of British shipping there.

At dawn on 13 December the Graf Spee was spotted at the river estuary. Lined up before it were the ships in Harwood's force; the heavy cruiser HMS Exeter, and two light cruisers, Ajax and Achilles, one from Britain and one from New Zealand.

CRUISERS DAMAGED

Graf Spee's captain, Hans Langsdorff, reckoned he could outgun the opposition, believing the heavy cruiser was accompanied only by destroyers. He opened fire, inflicting serious damage on the Exeter and the Ajax. The reply from the British ships crippled his own. With smoke pouring from the German ship, there was a chase led by the Graf Spee which was heading for the safety of Montevideo in Uruguay.

Although Uruguay was a neutral country, it was inclined to support the Allies. In international law, the Graf Spee was only entitled to stay in its capital, Montevideo, for 72 hours and the Uruguayans stoutly refused to extend its deadline.

It gave Langsdorff enough time to transfer his injured seamen to a German merchant ship. The most pressing repairs were carried out. But Langsdorff knew that outside the protection of Uruguyan territorial waters lurked a bevy a British ships waiting for a kill. Indeed, he believed the mighty Renown and Ark Royal had joined the pursuit when they were, in fact, hundreds of miles away.

Langsdorff deemed the situation hopeless and asked Berlin for permission to scuttle his ship, rather than have it fall in to enemy hands. Consent duly came.

Crowds had gathered on the waterfront eager to witness the great sea battle

On 17 December the Graf Spee set off slowly for the middle of the harbour. Crowds had gathered on the waterfront eager to witness the great sea battle that would surely follow. But they were disappointed. When the majority of the crew had safely disembarked, a huge explosion wrecked her and she sank to the estuary floor.

Langsdorff considered the incident a grave disgrace. Three days afterwards he wrapped himself in the flag of his beloved fatherland and put a bullet through his head.

NEUTRAL NORWAY

Churchill, First Lord of the Admiralty, instantly trumpeted the achievement of his navy even though it was gained by luck and misunderstanding on behalf of the enemy. Yet while Britain celebrated the triumph, it was far from the end of its troubles at sea.

Within a week in January three submarines, HMS Grenville and destroyer HMS Exmouth were sunk. There was little more by way of encouraging news for the British until February when HMS Cossack carried out a top secret raid on a German supply ship shelter in the waters of

EYE WITNESS

Bill Gamble, from Derbyshire, joined up in 1939 when he was 22. The following year, he became one of the thousands of men of the British Expeditionary Force evacuated from Dunkirk.

‘The Germans kept the beach under fire. I had never been under shell fire before. The Luftwaffe planes were strafing the beaches. There were rows and rows of fellows waiting to get on a boat. There was no panic because officers were there. They would have shot you if you had panicked.

I have got a vivid memory of the Welsh guards who formed the rear guard action which helped us escape. They were courageous men. I don't think I had properly fired a rifle until then. We didn't have half the equipment we should have had and there had been no training. We were just like civilians in uniform.

I was dead scared. Finally, I got on to a little barge and then on to a destroyer. When the waves came up we had to jump from one to the other. I landed in England on June 2. A few days later that destroyer got blown up. All those brave lads on the ship died.

At least when it came to D-Day, I wasn't bothered about it. By then I was properly trained. I had a job to do and I did it.’

Above: **With Hitler's consent the pocket battleship *Admiral Graf Spee* was spectacularly scuttled off Montevideo.**

neutral Norway. Aboard the *Altmark*, concealed in filthy conditions in a hold, were 300 prisoners taken by the *Graf Spee*. Regardless of international regulations which banned such action, the *Altmark* was boarded and the prisoners released. Norway protested about the violation of its neutrality. Its objections sounded somewhat lame, however, in the light of the fact that Norwegian authorities had apparently already searched the ship and apparently not found the captives. The daring feat persuaded Hitler that Norwegian waters should be under German control if his navy was to get the protection it deserved.

The Royal Navy continued its efforts to contain the U-boat threat and the activities of the German fleet until May 1940 when a task of much greater importance beckoned.

At the start of May, German forces had moved into Belgium. With characteristic speed, the Reich's forces overran Belgium, Holland and northern France. The lightning pace of the attack left everyone gasping for breath, not least the British Expeditionary Force, numbering some 200,000 men, which was sent to France at the outbreak of war to bolster French defences. The British soldiers were driven relentlessly back amid some bloody fighting. With them was a section of the French forces, weary and disenchanted with apparently no hope of escape.

The Reich's forces overran Belgium, Holland and northern France

Commander of the BEF, General Lord Gort, had quickly realised there was no option but to withdraw his men by sea. The best and shortest route would have been from Calais to Kent, but the French port was almost in the hands of the Germans already. Dunkirk seemed to be the single remaining point from which any kind of meaningful evacuation could take place.

British and French soldiers staggered on to the beach at Dunkirk in groups or sometimes singly. All semblance of order was gone after the hasty retreat in which bands of men lost sight of their units. Communication between commanders and their men was cut inland. The soldiers, now acting on initiative, got to Dunkirk as best they could.

The French forces' commander in chief, General Gamelin, had been bemused by the German advance. His tanks, evenly spaced down the frontier, were unable to provide a striking action against the rear of the Germans. So while the Panzer armies were tiring and running short of supplies, there was no one to exploit their vulnerability.

Ironically, it was Hitler himself who called a halt to the German

Right: The *Altmark* lurking in Norwegian waters was holding British POWs when HMS *Cossack* attacked.

march. Concerned that vital tank divisions were at risk if they went into action against the by-now concentrated strength of the Allies on treacherous marshlands and would be unable to complete the invasion of France, Hitler stopped the key Panzer advance. He was made even more anxious by the counter-offensive of sorts that the Allies had managed to stage at Arras.

DUNKIRK

The strategy was perhaps sound. Hitler's decision came on 24 May when a comprehensive rout of the enemy seemed assured. Its unavoidable side effect was to give Allied troops two days' grace without which an evacuation from Dunkirk would surely have been impossible. Historians have subsequently speculated that, had the BEF been lost in northern France, Britain would have sought peace at any price as there would have been no army left to fight with.

As early as 20 May, Admiral Bertram Ramsay, the Flag Officer at Dover, had been gathering a small fleet capable of crossing the English Channel to rescue soldiers. At this stage it was believed just 35,000 men would be saved.

Still more and more men were straggling on to the beach until the ragged throng numbered 38,000. Many were by now unarmed, picking up weapons where they could which had been discarded en route or fallen from the hands of recently killed comrades. There were still rations of sorts, but many soldiers had been without sleep for days. Between periods of calm and order there was panic as the instinct of self-preservation got the better of men with tattered nerves and a deep-rooted fear of what the future might hold if they were not rescued.

Each hour brought the Germans nearer. The shelling grew ever closer. Dunkirk itself was being blown to bits, offering little by way of protection for the British and French forces. There were attacks by the Luftwaffe, too. The low whine of oncoming aircraft followed by the clatter of its guns sent men diving to the ground for cover. Many never got up again.

'Operation Dynamo', the evacuation at Dunkirk, was officially begun on 26 May 1940

There was a feeling of resentment among many that the Royal Air Force was not doing its bit to aid the plight of the soldiers. In fact, its pilots were going up time and again, helping the rear guard defenders of Dunkirk or hampering the Luftwaffe high above the clouds. But the pilots' role was invisible to the eyes of the stranded soldiers – who were looking for someone to blame for their appalling predicament.

In peacetime Dunkirk had ample harbour facilities from which a major evacuation could have been carried out with ease. Now the town was rubble and the harbour installations in tatters. The only useful jetty left was wooden planking extending a mile into the sea. Yet it was valueless to the big ships for embarkation. Even the mildest wind would have blown the vessel into its concrete foundations causing damage below the waterline. As time went by it became clear that men would have to be taken off the beaches, no matter how cumbersome the task.

Operation Dynamo, the evacuation at Dunkirk, was officially begun shortly before 7pm on 26 May although in fact some support units had already been brought back to Britain. Before midnight fewer than 8,000 men had been brought home.

When the depth of the dilemma facing the bulk of Britain's army became clear, a flotilla of small boats was called upon to assist. Such boats already had to be registered with the government. Now they were recruited for the still-secret operation, with many civilian captains being allowed to stay with their ships.

The British public finally got to hear about 'Operation Dynamo' on

31 May, when about 194,000 British troops had been brought back under the guidance of the Royal Navy. When news about the crisis was broadcast, many more owners of small boats set sail immediately. This was the brave face of Dunkirk that haunts history.

CIVILIAN COURAGE

Their task was no easier than that faced by the Royal Navy. Bombardments by the Luftwaffe continued claiming the lives of servicemen and civilians alike. On 1 June the courage of the civilian boat owners reaped dividends when 64,429 soldiers were rescued. Having ferried their battle-worn cargo to safety, boat owners turned back to face the risks all over again in a bid to haul yet more soldiers to safety. Not least of their worries were the minefields that lay between them and their destination.

By any standards, the rout of the British army in France by Hitler's

The courage of the civilian boat owners reaped dividends

forces was nothing short of outright defeat. Yet the way in which the cream of the British army slipped through the Führer's grasp and the courage of the evacuation gave an element of heroism to the event, which set it apart from other ignominious military debacles suffered by the British, and has ensured it a special place in British military history.

The soldiers who made it back were full of criticism for the army that had sent them to France inadequately armed and supplied. Yet within a few days or weeks, most were posted again, in many cases back to France where remnants of the British contingent were still fighting with the French to keep Hitler out of Paris.

The last Allied boat pulled away from the beaches of Dunkirk on 4 June with the remnants of the 338,000 rescued British and French soldiers aboard. Each man was precious and represented the future fighting force of Britain. Yet behind the retreating force lay its equipment, without which no army could fight. Before leaving, the BEF had sabotaged 63,900 vehicles, 289 tanks and 2,472 guns.

◆ EYE WITNESS ◆

Miner Wilf Cowie was 25 when he joined the army and was part of the British Expeditionary Force in France which evacuated from Dunkirk.

"We were in France on the Belgian border for about six months with very little happening, just a bit of bombing and shelling.

When the retreat started, we had to make our way over fields because the Germans were patrolling the roads. The worst thing I ever saw were the refugees streaming out of Belgium pushing prams and carrying beds just machined gunned by German planes. Hundreds of them were killed.

I was one of the last to get out of Dunkirk. It was horrible on the beach. We were lying in bomb craters on the beach, expecting every day to get away. Every day seemed to take forever. Luftwaffe planes were firing at us and then there was the shelling. That was the worst thing of all. The shells screamed as they were going over the top of you and you never knew where they were going to land.

Once I took shelter in a bomb hole with three other lads. I was the only one who came out alive. The others were killed by a machine gun blast from an aeroplane.

There were hundreds of lads killed. We had to go and get the identity discs from the bodies and give them to our superiors. It was a bit upsetting but it was just a job that had to be done. We saw so many young men dead that in the end we didn't worry about it.

I came back in a trawler. It took 36 hours to reach the east coast after the skipper diverted to avoid mines. Several men on the boat died when they were hit by machine gun fire from Luftwaffe planes passing overhead."

Above: **Devastation of the beaches of Dunkirk following the evacuation.**

U-BOAT MENACE

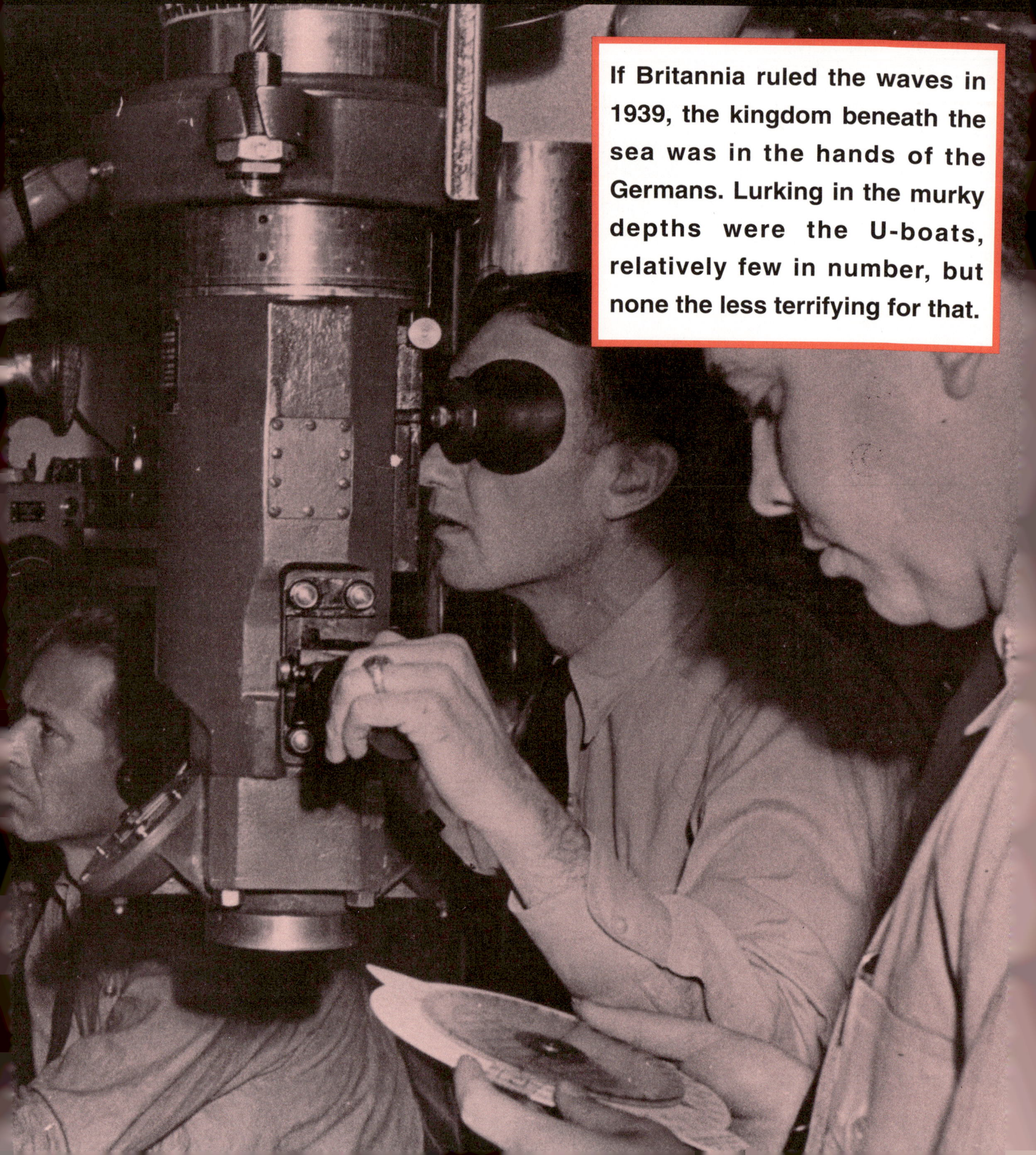

If Britannia ruled the waves in 1939, the kingdom beneath the sea was in the hands of the Germans. Lurking in the murky depths were the U-boats, relatively few in number, but none the less terrifying for that.

Just a mention of the name could strike fear into the stout hearts of the English sailors. Winston Churchill confessed later that the U-boat threat in the Battle of the Atlantic was 'the only thing that ever really frightened me during the war'.

Above: German U-boats came close to their goal of strangling Britain.

For U-boats (Unterseeboot in German) had a habit of creeping up on British shipping and sinking it without warning. At first merchant ships seemed very much like sitting ducks if U-boats were in the area. There appeared to be little opportunity to dilute the threat.

Britain, Canada and America lost thousands of tons of cargo, not to mention scores of seamen, to the prowling U-boats. Bitter experience finally taught the Allies effective defences and, later, vital offensive tactics which would ultimately neutralise the stealthy foe.

U-boats soon began to hunt in 'wolf packs', an idea thought up in Germany in the mid-1930s in which a group of submarines orchestrated their attacks on convoys. At first, the concept was thwarted by a lack of boats. Sometimes, in the early stages of the war, there were only a handful of submarines to put to sea, the others being in dock for repairs or in use for training. The lack of air support from the Luftwaffe to the U-boat service also slightly lessened their menace, since they were compelled to search, sometimes for days, for convoys.

Above: Admiral Karl Dönitz knew the potential of his U-boat fleet. *Left:* The Allies also had submarines.

By the summer of 1940 there were two 'wolf packs' operating in the Atlantic

However Raeder, commander in chief of the Kriegsmarine was conscious of the golden opportunity that was open to him. While finding it almost impossible to keep more than six U-boats in the sea at a time before February 1941, he devoted much time and energy to rectifying the short-coming. Before the year was out the number of U-boats in his fleet had been increased tenfold.

By the summer of 1940 there were two wolf packs operating in the Atlantic, preying on the convoys as they made their way with precious food, goods and, later, troops to Britain from America. Submarine commanders could now pinpoint convoy positions thanks to the German Radio Monitoring Service (B-Dienst). Slung across the Atlantic, the U-boats formed a deadly chain from which the convoys could not escape. The aim was for the boat which first spotted the convoy to shadow it until other submarines could gather for a mass attack. In October, three convoys lost 38 ships to U-boats in the space of just three nights.

U-BOAT TECHNIQUE

The technique used by the U-boats continued to improve. At first, commanders attacked from positions both above and below the waves. Their firepower was far more accurate, however, when the U-boats were on the surface. It became

accepted procedure for the boats to sneak into the centre of a convoy, surface after dark and wreak havoc, disappearing before daybreak when the first of the Allied flight escorts arrived. On the surface, the sleek machines, powered by diesel engines, could outrun larger convoy escort vessels with relative ease.

On the surface, the sleek machines could outrun larger convoy escort vessels

There followed a 'happy time', as it was known among German submariners, in which dozens of merchant ships were sent to the bottom. They were picking off targets with ease and the convoy escorts were floundering with exasperation, not knowing how to halt the rising casualty toll. In 1940, U-boats accounted for more than 1,000 ships while just 16 U-boats were knocked out. The following year followed a similar pattern with 24 U-boats being sunk.

AMPLE WARNING

Had there been a greater number of U-boats operating at that time, Britain would have been in grave danger of being throttled. Hitler was delighted with the success of the U-boats. Always sceptical of the power of his naval fleet, he became a convert and lavished his favours on the U-boat arm. If he had devoted more resources to them in 1939 instead of waiting until 1941, the outcome of the war might have been very different. By the time his confidence was raised in the potential of the U-boats, it was just one of many services forced to get in line for the available resources.

Above: **One U-boat torpedo was enough to break a ship's back.**

Right: **Sailors keeping watch from a surfaced submarine got a drenching.**

As it was, technology came to the rescue for the Allies. Britain finally cracked the German radio code signals. Now operators could give ample warning to the convoys as to the whereabouts of the U-boats. Ships began to successfully bypass the waiting packs which were now forced to stretch out over huge distances, diminishing their effect.

Operators could give ample warning as to the whereabouts of the U-boats

Although the sinking of the liner Athenia at the beginning of the war did serve to tighten up the rules of engagement which governed U-boats, these were soon relaxed, in part because it was difficult for submariners to abide by such rules without putting themselves into considerable danger. Stipulations like the one laid down in the 1935 London Submarine Agreement that submarines must stop intended victims and order the crew into lifeboats before opening fire were soon forgotten. The hunter quickly became the hunted if he lingered too long trying to establish the identity and purpose of a ship in the Atlantic. Neutral shipping was also at risk

◆ EYE WITNESS ◆

The following personal account of life aboard a patrolling British submarine in the Mediterranean appeared in the *Daily Express* in June 1942.

"The captain is wearing shorts with a sweater handy in case it is chilly. His favourite dress while submerged in action is a towel wrapped around his loins.

The crew are wearing overalls, shorts, shirts, vests – anything they fancy. There are no badges of rank and it is impossible to tell the captain from the cook.

Life goes on quietly, almost dully, for some days while the submarine continues towards her patrol station. There are only seven gramophone records, some of them scratched and indistinct through constant wear. The captain tells the first lieutenant he will brain the first rating to play *Frankie and Johnnie were lovers* – he swears he has heard it 3,000 times.

At midday the next day the captain is resting in his cabin. The first lieutenant is at the periscope. He swings it, sees smoke on the horizon. Without ceasing to look he says: "Captain, in the control room". The murmur is taken up and goes around the boat. Within a matter of seconds the captain is at the periscope clothed in his towel. He looks and says: "There is smoke on the horizon – a couple of masts."

Then the orders come fast. "Diving stations, full speed ahead together, starboard 25, steer 320." The hum of the motors can be heard through the otherwise silent submarine.

There are three merchant ships escorted by six Italian destroyers. The captain grabs his slipping towel as he snaps the range – 8,000 yards.

Excitement in the submarine is terrific and suppressed. Nobody speaks except the captain. At times the silence is so intense that a movement by a rating sounds like thunder.

As the torpedoes jump from the tubes the submarine shudders a bit. The captain's towel falls off. Nearby ratings chuckle at naked authority.

Stop watches have already started to mark the time the torpedoes take to reach the target. The captain's: "I'll have a cup of tea, please," is hardly necessary. The electric stove was switched on some minutes before. It is a ritual. Everybody in the service knows that you must have a cup of tea before the depth charging begins.

In 55 seconds the explosion which means the target has been hit rocks the submarine. The captain sits on the engine-room artificer's tool box, sipping his tea. Then the first depth charge arrives.

The captain's cup leaps off the tool chest. The submarine vibrates with the clangour of charges exploding nearby.

For two hours the racket of the depth charges goes on. The men behave as if they were on tiptoe. Barely a word is spoken. As the noise of the depth charges dies away the submarine creeps to periscope depth. The captain sees three destroyers picking up survivors from the sunken merchantmen.

One of the ratings off duty has already got hold of the "Jolly Roger" skull and cross bones flag of the submarine service and is preparing to stitch another chevron to the other battle honours. They will fly it when they get back from patrol."

Below: In 1942 the remains of a convoy approach beseiged Malta.

Above: **Relief as a German U-boat and its crew return safely to port after a long spell on patrol.**

from German U-boats. Some vessels flying the flags of unaligned countries were hit by accident. Others, suspected of aiding the British, were rammed or torpedoed on purpose.

In November 1939 neutral countries were warned by Germany that their ships could not be guaranteed a safe passage in waters around the British Isles. Meanwhile, secret instructions to U-boat commanders gave them the go-ahead to sink tankers and other key commercial ships approaching Britain unless they were identified as Russian, Japanese, Italian, Spanish, Greek or American. To cover their tracks, the U-boat commanders were told to use only electric torpedoes which did not leave a tell-tale wake in the water. It meant the explosion could be blamed on an engine fault or a mine.

It wasn't only in the Atlantic that the U-boats plied their deadly trade. Six were broken into pieces and transported by road to Linz in Austria where the water was deep enough for re-assembly and were then launched into the Black Sea. The first to go into action there took to the water on 28 October 1940.

Operation in the Mediterranean was difficult for the U-boats – which were known by numbers rather than names – as their dark forms could be quickly spotted in the shallow, clear water by aircraft above or nearby ships. Also, the fast flowing eastern currents assisted the U-boats as they

It wasn't only in the Atlantic that the U-boats plied their deadly trade

sailed into the warm seas but thwarted their exit.

Nevertheless, it was there that the U81 sank HMS Ark Royal on 13 November 1941, one of the prestige ships of the Royal Navy.

Far easier was the task of the U-boats in the waters off America and Canada. Until Japan's attack on Pearl Harbor and Germany's subsequent declaration of war on America, Hitler had ordered that any ship bearing the stars and stripes standard be allowed freedom of the waters. There had been sinkings of US vessels before December 1941, but presumably these were in error.

When America and Germany were eventually pitted against each other, the U-boats seized the opportunity for yet another 'happy time'. U-boat commander in chief Karl Dönitz, the man who was later to take over from Hitler as Führer of Germany, knew his forces had to pounce before America became wise to the threat.

Five of the largest submarines, called Type IX boats, were dispatched from the Mediterranean

EYE WITNESS

Stoker Fernand 'Pedro' Guinard, 69, from Halifax, Nova Scotia, served on several Canadian warships including HMCS *St. Laurent*.

My first contact with the enemy came early in the war when we picked up 27 survivors from the German submarine UB31. We were four days out of Newfoundland.

A lot of these guys were Czechs and Poles. They told me they'd been offered the chance to fight in the navy or go work in a slave camp. You couldn't really blame them for joining up. I got quite close to them because I had to detail them to hand pump the bilges.

Even that got me into trouble. When we docked and disembarked the POWs, two of the Germans came over to shake hands and say goodbye. That didn't go down well with the officers. I got warned in no uncertain terms not to fraternise with the prisoners.

We only killed one submarine in my first three years of service. But we saw plenty of attacks on our convoys. I remember one time when a wolf pack began torpedoing our boats at sunset. It was so sad to see these ships going down. There were people in the water everywhere but to be honest we didn't give a bag about them. There were guys in a life raft obviously looking for help and we just rode straight through them throwing out depth charges. All we cared about was getting the submarine.

Was I scared? I didn't have much time to be scared. I was part of a team and you just got on with your job.

where they were then operating to North American coastal waters in 'Operation Paukenschlag'.

EASY TARGETS

Americans living along the eastern seaboard had so far been virtually untouched by the war. There were no blackouts, built-in defences, or restrictions on radio use. Even navigation lights remained helpfully in place. Not only did the U-boats have easy targets but, after the 'kill', the pursuing submarine hunters were inexperienced and ill-prepared. There was little to stop the U-boats getting clean away. In 'Operation Paukenschlag', each boat averaged almost six 'kills' before returning to home waters. Some of the boats sunk were those who had traversed the Atlantic in a convoy to pick up a cargo only to be sunk, as the British saw it, through a reckless lack of defence on behalf of the Americans.

A further wave of 12 smaller boats did their utmost to match the grand total but, thankfully for the Americans, fell short of the target. Within a few months, America began using convoy systems in its home waters and mimicked the successful British methods of hunting U-boats.

The tentacles of the U-boat campaign also spread into the southern oceans. There were plenty of ships carrying essential goods which

Within a few months, America began using convoy systems in its home waters

Below: **Living conditions on a U-boat were cramped and uncomfortable, with restricted fresh food and air.**

were poorly equipped to deal with U-boat attack. In addition, it further stretched the Royal Navy ships charged with hunting for submarines.

Not all of the 1,300 U-boats put to see by Germany during World War II saw action. Some were used for training, others for supplying the roving hunters. Still more U-boats were employed carrying goods from the far east to the Fatherland.

U-boat men got about double the rates of pay awarded to other sailors

Above: **A U-boat in harbour is loaded with supplies before embarking on another lengthy ship-bagging voyage.**

Men who served in the U-boat arm of the Kriegsmarine (German Navy) were considered the elite by their countrymen – although they were loathed and detested by the British. There can be little doubt that they had strong nerves and plenty of courage. Some were volunteers, attracted by the excitement the service appeared to offer. This was perpetuated by the public accolades awarded to U-boat aces like Gunther Prien and Joachim Schepke. U-boat men also got about double the rates of pay awarded to other sailors. Other men who found themselves serving on the U-boats were naval recruits who had been drafted.

Yet aboard a U-boat, the day-to-day life was far from glamorous. Conditions were cramped. There was a curtained-off cabin for the captain but there were not enough beds for every member of the crew. Some men slept in hammocks, while others slept on the floor.

MASCOTS

Animals featured as mascots to the branches of army, navy and air force throughout the war. On HMS *Duke of York*, the ship's tabby cat was Whiskey who became famous for sleeping soundly through the battle which sunk the Scharnhorst. A cat called Susan made herself at home on a Royal Navy tank landing craft and even attended the D-Day invasion. A St Bernard by the name of Bamse was the mascot of the Norwegian fighting ship *Thorod*. He assured himself a place in the heart of his crew by rounding them up from shore leave by visiting their favourite bars and clubs – even boarding a bus to patrol the more far-reaching destinations.

One of the more unusual mascots of the war was a Syrian bear by the name of Voytek, adopted as a cub by the Second Polish Transport Company in Persia. He was thought of as human by his soldier pals who watched distressed as he cried like a child when his carer, Lance Corporal Peter Prendys, disappeared from sight. His love of water led to the shower room having to be locked to prevent him from exhausting the water supply. When he discovered an Arab spy, he was acclaimed a hero and allowed a morning's free play in the bath.

It was as a hero he was greeted in Scotland at the end of the war where he served the army until 1947 when his owner was demobbed. It was then he was handed over to Edinburgh Zoo where he had to get used to a new life behind bars.

LIFE EXPECTANCY

Until hostilities began with America, the U-boat commanders had little idea of the distances their crafts were able to travel. They were pleasantly surprised to find they could cruise far further than they ever thought possible if they conserved fuel by keeping to reasonable speeds and travelled on the surface.

More supplies were needed on a long voyage, however. They took up valuable living accommodation, leaving the crew of about 50 even fewer comforts. Water was rationed nd the opportunities for washing ɿere few. The atmosphere was qualid, sweaty and unpleasant.

Early models were even more partan than the rest. There was nadequate heating aboard. So men oaked from taking their turn on the vatch when the boat was on the urface found themselves unable to lry their sodden clothes. Men wore ayers of jumpers and still felt chilled.

When the most primitive U-boats were forced to submerge, the men

Above: **A U-boat is armed with a giant torpedo before a trip.**
Left: **Sailors stood little chance when a U-boat was blown up.**

had to wear breathing masks to prevent poisoning by carbon monoxide. Later, more sophisticated air purifiers were built into the wall of the ships, so masks became obselete.

Voyages lasted for months at a time and there was little chance to

The greatest shadow over a U-boat crewman was his brief life expectancy

breath fresh air. U-boat men operating in the darkened Arctic region during the winter months were known to queue up patiently for a glimpse of sunlight.

Perhaps the greatest shadow over the life of a U-boat crewman, though, was his brief life expectancy.

During the first two years of war, their existence was perilous due

Left: **Depth charges were one antidote to roaming U-boats.**

entirely to the shortcomings in their torpedo systems. Then, when they bore the brunt of Allied air and sea power, U-boats became an endangered species. Apart from torpedoes and mines, the only weapon the U-boats could use against their enemies was an undersized machine gun which could do little in the face of a concerted attack. German sailors grew into the habit of calling their craft 'iron coffins'.

German sailors grew into the habit of calling their craft 'iron coffins'

After attacking, there are examples of U-boat captains displaying concern for their victims, passing on food and water and radioing their position so help could be sent. Survivors were never allowed on board, however.

Equally, there were tales that abounded in Britain of men from sunken ships being machine-gunned to death by callous U-boat captains as they lay helpless in the water. While that may have occurred, there is the strong possibility such stories were used for propaganda purposes by a Ministry of Information which depicted U-boat captains as callous, dedicated Nazis.

The most successful U-boat was U48, which came into service in April 1939 and sank a record 59 ships before being sunk itself in October 1943. Many of the submarines, particularly those commissioned in the later years of the war, sunk five or fewer ships, many making no hits at all before they were sent to the ocean bed.

The U-boat force gradually became more impotent prompting the desperate Dönitz, by now admiral of the entire Kriegsmarine, to order a kamikaze-style attack by them following D-Day.

RECKLESS ATTACK

On 11 June 1944 he issued an order which read: 'The Invasion Fleet is to be attacked with complete recklessness. Every enemy vessel that aids the landing, even if it puts no more than half a hundred men or a tank ashore, is a target calling for all-out effort from the U-boat.

'It is to be attacked even at the risk of losing one's boat. When it is necessary to get to grips with the enemy landing fleet, there is no question of any regard to danger through shallow water or possible minefields.'

Even with the benefit of hindsight it is difficult to discern whether the U-boat captains, fired by their leader's words, carried out assaults

ORAN DILEMMA

In one of the most controversial moves of the war, Churchill turned British guns against former ally France a little more than a week after the armistice with Germany was signed.

A British squadron led by Vice Admiral James Somerville encircled the pride of the French fleet harboured in the Algerian port of Oran on 3 July 1940 as part of 'Operation Catapult' and issued an ultimatum to the ships sheltering there to sail for Britain or America. When the order was refused, the mighty force of British ships including the ill-fated battlecruiser *Hood* opened fire.

Prestige ships, among them the *Provence*, *Bretagne* and *Dunkerque* were sunk or badly damaged and 1,300 French sailors were killed. The aim was to prevent the ships falling into German hands but it caused a major outcry in France and among French-speaking nations around the world.

Churchill said he regretted the loss of life but insisted the action was necessary. 'I leave the judgement of our actions with confidence to Parliament. I leave it to the nation and I leave it to the United States. I leave it to the world and to history.'

The French ships in British ports were confiscated with barely one shot being fired.

and were defeated or if indeed the U-boat force was already so depleted and poorly supplied that they were unable to take any meaningful action. Certainly, there is little evidence of U-boat activity in the Channel following D-Day.

Despite the Allied successes in combatting the U-boat menace, the Nazi hierarchy continued to pin great hopes on the success of a renewed campaign. Hitler, keeping faith with the U-boat service, was convinced the newest model designed by Germany was a war-winner. In his diaries, dated 6 March 1945, his loyal aide Goebbels reflected those optimistic opinions. With the Allies crossing the borders of Germany into the Fatherland itself, he wrote: 'There is considerable hope for us here. Our U-boats must get to work hard; above all it may be anticipated that as the new type gets into action, far greater results should be achieved than with our old U-boats . . .'

Later, on 28 March, barely a month before the collapse of Hitler's Germany, he noted the Allied bombing campaign against the new submarines in dock at Bremen and penned with satisfaction: 'Clearly the revival of our U-boat war has made a great impression on the war.'

Above: **U-boat construction sites became priority targets for Allied air forces.**

Below: **Another convoy ship falls victim of U-boats, Hitler's underused war weapon.**

BATTLE OF THE ATLANTIC

During World War I, German U-boats almost succeeded in severing the supply routes from America and Canada to Britain. Without shiploads of goods, including fuel, from overseas the prospects for Britain were dim.

Unable to support herself, Britain had for years relied on trade to keep her people fed, othed and employed. If those vital nks were cut during conflict, Britain ould have been forced to capitulate – r see her population starve. Now in Vorld War II the grim scenario was eing played out once more. U-boats, n tandem with the German Navy or Kriegsmarine, were set to exploit the Achilles heel of the British Empire. They nearly succeeded.

Both Britain and Germany's navies had been unprepared for war. Navy chief Erich Raeder had far fewer U-boats at his disposal than he would have liked. In addition, the submarine construction programme was virtually at a halt. Hitler had little faith in his navy and earmarked only limited resources for it.

Meanwhile, Britain had a mighty fleet of Royal Navy vessels and numerous merchant ships. But the Admiralty appeared to have devoted little time or effort in the years between the wars in looking at ways to counter the U-boat threat. It still believed in the outdated notion that wars could be won with offensive action by battleships.

Putting their lives on the line alongside sailors in the Royal Navy were volunteer merchant seamen. It was their job to ferry the all-important supplies to Britain, mostly from America and Canada across the Atlantic. Instantly, they became targets for the roaming U-boats. Their pay was £9 a month with an additional two shillings and sixpence in danger money.

Instantly, the convoy system in which merchant ships banded together and travelled under armed escort was employed once again, as it had been with marked success in World War I. There were some drawbacks, however, which made shortages more acute on the homefront. For example, it took valuable time for a convoy to be assembled and some ships were compelled to travel by a longer route than they otherwise would have done. Speedier ships were impeded by the pace of slower vessels. Also, dockyards became hopelessly congested when a glut of ships arrived all at once.

The major threat in the Atlantic was always from U-boats

ESCORT SHIPS

Nevertheless, the accompanying Royal Navy ships at least offered some protection to the merchant fleet. At first, however, the short range of the accompanying ships meant that escorts could only be offered for some 200 miles out of Britain. The convoy was then on its own until it met with a reciprocal Canadian escort a few hundred miles from the other side. It offered a mid-Atlantic gap which was ideal for hunter U-boats.

Even the proximity of the armed destroyers at the outset and close of the voyages proved little deterrent to the U-boats in the opening years of World War II.

The major threat in the Atlantic was always from U-boats and sometimes from merchant ships fitted out with weaponry, known as armed

Left: **Freezing weather in the Atlantic had the crew thawing out anchor chains.**
Below: **U-boats on far-flung missions were dependent on supply ships.**

raiders. Hitler was unwilling to risk his capital ships in the open sea after the Bismarck disaster. Lacking any aircraft carriers, the Germans were unable to launch air bombardments out of range of their airfields.

If they operated at night, the U-boats often went unnoticed by the escort ships even on the surface. Low in the water and much smaller than a surface ship, the most vigilant watch could be forgiven for letting the streamline craft slip by.

By the close of 1940, more than 4,700,000 tons of British shipping had been lost

The only technology available to counter the threat from U-boats was Asdic, a sonar device which sent out underwater impulses that could, by the sound of the echoes, indicate the presence of solid objects. Not only was it almost useless used at speed or against surface objects, but early models were also unable to produce an accurate range and operators were woefully inexperienced.

In a bid to flush out U-boats during the early months of the war, Royal Navy warships attempted sweeps of convoy routes. The U-boats would simply dive and wait for the danger to pass. Even if their presence was detected, there was every chance the depth charge dropped by a pursuing vessel would fall short of its intended mark.

As the war progressed, Germany eased the way for its U-boat captains in their task of sinking trans-Atlantic shipping by providing new ports from which they could operate. The fall of Norway and France offered plenty of fresh and friendly harbours for repairs and restocking. In por the U-boats were housed in speciall built bunkers with two metre thic walls. That meant that although th docks came under heavy fire durin Allied bombing raids the U-boat remained safe. It wasn't until 194 that the Allies found sufficient fir power to shatter these solid defences.

By the close of 1940, more thar 4,700,000 tons of British shipping had been lost in the form of 1,281 vessels, about one fifth of the pre-war merchant fleet.

EYE WITNESS

Dennis Bell, 67, of Waterlooville, Hampshire, was one of the youngest seamen to sail with the D-Day invasion fleet. At 16 he was a galley boy in the merchant navy, serving aboard the converted troop ship *Liberation of Europe*. His pay was £2 per week , including £1 3s 4d 'war risk money'.

I spent the early months of 1944 chugging along the south coast to drop off soldiers for secret beach-storming exercises. Looking back, I was incredibly naive about the whole business of war. I was only a kid and I knew nothing. I used to think I'd be all right because I was wearing my lifejacket.

By D-Day I'd already had a taste of the Atlantic War. At 15 I was galley boy aboard a crude carrier called the *Robert F. Hind*, bringing oil from the States to Britain and North Africa. Nobody would ever tell me what was going on – they would just shout at me to get back to the galley and work.

I soon cottoned on to the fact that none of the escort ships wanted to come too close to us. Obviously a tanker was a nice juicy target for the U-boats and if we'd gone up in flames we'd have lit up the sky.

Left: **Crewmen on board an escort warship observe the progress of a southbound convoy.**

Above: **Always alert, seamen knew the threat of attack was never far away.**
Right: **Germany housed her precious U-boats in sturdy concrete bunkers.**

In May 1941, the first convoy to receive protection for the entirety of its voyage set sail. It was an important first step towards victory in the Battle of the Atlantic.

Soon after came the introduction of radar, still far from foolproof but a huge boon to the navy ships charged with spotting predators. Radar also aided Coastal Command aircraft as to the whereabouts of U-boats. Now, at last, aircraft could be brought to bear against the undersea menace and the planes posted to coastal duties appeared to be reaping a reward. Britain's Admiralty, without a fleet air arm, was constantly battling to keep those few planes in place when many in the RAF and the war office thought they would be better employed bombing land-based targets in Europe. It took several years for the Germans in command to become fully aware of the danger posed by radar to its U-boats.

Now, at last, aircraft could be brought to bear against the undersea menace

Also, the British cashed in on a fatal flaw of the wolf pack system used by U-boats, in which a handful of craft operated together during a convoy attack. To alert nearby boats of the presence of a convoy, the German commanders had to use their radios. The prospect of the British being able to track the signals was dismissed out of hand by the Germans for months. But that is just what did happen when the High Frequency Direction Finder was pioneered, affectionately known as

Above: A US destroyer pulls alongside HMS *Norfolk* to refuel mid-voyage.

'Huff-duff'. When the U-boat position was fixed by the radio operators, it gave Royal Navy vessels far greater scope in their attack.

Convoy defences were reorganised so that extra escort boats could loiter above a submerged submarine for up to two days, waiting for the craft to surface for air. Then it was an easy target. Other vessels manoeuvred themselves around the precious convoy ships to fill the gap left by the lingering vessel for fear that another U-boat would make merry in the unexpected opening.

1941 proved to be a key year for the Allies in their fight against the U-boats

In the British armoury, too, was the increasing ability of the decoders to pinpoint the position of U-boats. At the start of the war, the translation of the messages sent between the German admiralty and its ships was slow and provided only retrospective information. With practice, the 'tapping' system speeded up, providing accurate and detailed assistance for convoys and British ships on the whereabouts of the enemy. While the German commanders suspected a breach in security, they never identified where the leak was.

So 1941 proved to be a key year for the Allies in their fight against the U-boats. Although 432 ships were sunk, the total was down on the previous year. The U-boat arm lost 35 of its craft.

When the U-boats turned their attentions to the pickings off America in early 1942, the pressure on the Atlantic convoys eased. But when the U-boats returned to Atlantic waters, it was with a vengeance.

AIRCRAFT ATTACKS

At last U-boat manufacture was coming up to the levels hoped for by Dönitz. Every month, 20 new U-boats left the ship yards.

The boost for the Kriegsmarine was bad news for British sailors in the Atlantic who found themselves

EYE WITNESS

Forbes Brown, from Victoria, British Columbia, joined the Royal Canadian Navy in 1941, training as an Asdic operator.

Being a Canadian ship, we didn't drink much tea. When we were docked in Londonderry, my pal Bob took me to see 'Black Dan'. He sold 'Black Dan' an enormous box of tea for £1. Bob took the money and later that night tied the box of tea to a rope and lowered it down the side of the ship to the dockside where Dan was waiting.

When I next went ashore, Bob asked me to find 'Black Dan' and offer him a bag of sugar for £1. When Dan came to collect the sugar he tasted it before handing over the money to Bob and making off.

Two nights later I was on gang plank duty when Bob was brought back with a great gash in his head. He had concussion and was severely bruised up. I went to see him later on.

He confessed there was only a fraction of sugar in the bag he had sold 'Black Dan'. The rest was salt, dirt cheap even then. I never went back to see 'Black Dan' again after that and neither did Bob.

once more at the heart of a fierce battle for survival. Although the extended air patrols aided the safety of the ships and significantly improved the rate at which U-boats were knocked out, it was still a fearful fight to the death. U-boats began to attack once more during daylight hours, a sign of their boosted confidence.

During August and September alone U-boats – helped by the German advances in cracking British codes – found 21 convoys and sank 43 ships. By the end of 1942 Allied tonnage totalling 7,500,000 had been sunk, more than the combined totals for the three previous years of war.

Above: **When a convoy put to sea, the Atlantic throbbed with activity.**

Allied aircraft stepped up the numbers of attacks against U-boats during 1943 after the long-awaited allocation of more long-range aircraft. Between March 1943 and the end of the war, air attack accounted for 290 U-boats alone. A surface U-boat could offer little by way of defence to an aircraft as its guns were so small as to be useless.

Between March 1943 and the end of the war, air attack accounted for 290 U-boats

Below: **A cargo ship is lost amid smoke and flames following an air attack.**

Suddenly, the campaign against U-boats was accelerating. That spring eight U-boats were lost in the battle to protect one convoy. During May alone 41 were sent to the bottom of the ocean, causing a concerned Dönitz to pull the ranks of remaining U-boats out of the Atlantic for a few months. Still, he failed to question the security of his cipher system.

The importance of the Battle of the Atlantic suddenly loomed large for Hitler

The importance of the Battle of the Atlantic suddenly loomed large for Hitler, who had previously been wholly absorbed in his bid to conquer Russia.

In January 1943 Admiral Raeder was replaced as commander in chief of the Kriegsmarine by Dönitz. Hitler saw Dönitz with new eyes after the impressive successes of the U-boat war. Now Dönitz found it impossible to achieve similar standards.

U-boat production was still relatively healthy, despite an increasing shortage of manpower in the dockyards. However, the lack of crews was becoming a dilemma for Dönitz who was compelled to send barely trained men into action despite the fact he believed the success of the U-boats lay at least in part with a rigorous training for the men aboard.

LIBERTY SHIPS

The Allies, meanwhile, had the bonus of Liberty ships – rapidly made craft which went to replace the mercantile fleet decimated by U-boat action. By July 1943, the number of new ships coming out of the American yards

EYE WITNESS

Swedish-born Nels Olson, 72, from Chicago, USA, was a gunner in the US Navy Armed Guard, responsible for manning 5-inch guns on Atlantic convoy merchant ships.

"There were 1800 of us in the Armed Guard and they split us up to around 25 per ship. I signed up in December 1942 and was assigned to the *Alcobanner*, built during World War I. Later I moved on to Liberty ships. The US built 2,700 of these during the war and it was just as well because the Germans sank so many. I guess we lost nearly 800 in the first eight months.

The Armed Guard took heavier losses than any other US naval unit. Merchant ships were a prime target because there was so little with which to defend them. We knew it was bad when we volunteered. They only took volunteers. No one was ordered to do it.

When the German submarines got in among a convoy it was a terrible sight. They always attacked at night and there was always pandemonium. I remember watching an oil tanker explode. It lit up the skies for miles around. And we had no target to fire back at."

Left: **Young, fit men were always needed for the fight against the U-boats.**

was greater in total than the amount being lost.

With losses being so severe, the pack formation was abandoned in the autumn of 1943 and U-boats returned to the Atlantic hunting alone, cutting their effectiveness.

In looking at the Battle of the Atlantic, it is important to remember the contribution made by Britain's own submarines. During the war they sank 15 U-boats. Only three British U-boats were sent to the bottom by U-boats. Submarines were never sighted by their own kind until they were at very close range. For a successful attack to be presse home, the two could be no more than half a mile apart. The first U-boat fell victim to HMS Salmon as early as December 1939.

COST OF CONFLICT

In the last four months of 1943, the U-boats succeeded in sinking 67 ships at a cost of 64 U-boats. Clearly, the Battle of the Atlantic was lost by the Germans although it would be months before shipping in the Atlantic was completely safe from U-boat attack.

Above: **A convoy reaches port, thanks this time to the Royal Canadian Navy.**

◆ EYE WITNESS ◆

J. H. Blonk, from Eindhoven, Holland, was blinded in one eye in 1941 when he was serving as an engineer on the cargo ship *de Friesland* which was hit off the English coast.

"We knew that if we were hit, we were on our own – the other ships would not and were not allowed to turn back otherwise they would be easy targets. The ship saunk so fast that we didn't even manage to get a float from the deck.

I can still remember how the wireless operator who I shared a cabin with was standing beside me. Then the water came and I never saw him again, I just felt his hand on my leg.

I was in the water for four hours. I held on to a panel from the deck that had gone overboard. An English communications officer was holding on to the other side. After an hour or so he said to me: "I think I'm going to let myself go, I'm so tired, I can't hang on any more."

I begged him to keep going. After he went, I lost all conception of time and that is the greatest danger for a drowning man – he thinks he is bobbing around for hours when in reality it is a much shorter time.

After four hours a trawler returned from the convoy to see if there were any survivors. Thirteen members of a 27-man crew were saved."

At the end of the war, it became clear that the conflicts at sea – chiefly the Battle of the Atlantic – had been costly for both sides.

During the war, the Allies lost 5,150 merchant ships, 2,828 of them to U-boats. The number of merchant seamen who lost their lives amounted to 50,000. The U-boat tally also included 148 Allied warships.

As for the U-boat arm, 785 of its 1,131 strong fleet were lost, costing the lives of at least 27,491 crew and officers. About 5,000 were taken prisoners of war.

MATAPAN

Jostling for pole position in the Mediterranean, the tussle between the Italian and British navies was set to be of epic proportions. In the event, the British navy pulled off a tactical masterstroke which decided the debate before Italy marked its first anniversary at war.

Britain had its own Mediterranean fleet. Key bases for Britain were Gibraltar, at the teeth of the Mediterranean, the hard-pressed island of Malta and Alexandria, the Egyptian port operating under Admiral Sir Andrew Cunningham, from which supplies were being shipped to Greece.

Italy had well-established ports of its home territory opening into the Mediterranean and the Aegean as well as control of Albania and Libya, on the northern coast of Africa.

When war broke out, the British had a grasp of Italian naval codes and gathered enough information to sink nine Italian submarines before the end of June 1940. But a fortuitous switch in cipher systems by the Italians in July prevented the British from cracking the codes again.

The Italian air force wasted no time in bombing the British big ships when they were at sea. Italian intelligence about British sea traffic was good. It enabled her captains to circumnavigate all convoys to Libya around the British forces.

The Italian air force wasted no time in bombing the British big ships

Against this background, Cunningham was determined to punish his Italian enemies and put to sea 16 times between June and October 1940. Yet he only managed to track Mussolini's ships three times.

So it was a priceless morale booster for the British when, on 11 November 1940, the Fleet Air Arm attacked Taranto, an Italian port. In port were six Italian battleships. A dozen Swordfish aircraft from the aircraft carrier Illustrious took off at dusk and flew 170 miles to deal the blow to the Italian navy vessels, struggling to gain height with their heavy load of explosives.

They notched up two strikes with hits against the battleships Cavour and Littorio. A second wave of Swordfish arrived less than an hour afterwards, directed to their target by the blaze now roaring at the base. Together, they damaged the battleship Duilio. At a cost of two aircraft, the Italian fleet was deprived of three valuable battleships – Cavour permanently; Littorio and Duilio until the late spring of 1941.

The Italian navy was still a force to be reckoned with, however. Admiral Cunningham was determined the threat they posed to Allied shipping in the Mediterranean should be rubbed out.

At the turn of the year, Fliegerkorps X, the Luftwaffe's anti-shipping force, transferred 200 of its aircraft to Sicily. By 10 January 1941 bombers from the precision corps landed six bombs on Illustrious and also struck Warspite, although neither ship was terminally damaged.

It demonstrated, however, the need for air superiority if the Allies were to control the Mediterranean. Unfortunately, there was a shortage of Allied aircraft in the area, worsened when the Illustrious was hit again while in dock at Malta. Air attacks against Malta were so heavy and so frequent that it proved impossible to carry out adequate repairs to the much-needed aircraft carrier there. Consequently she had to be withdrawn from the Mediterranean.

ITALIAN THREAT

The British resolve to eradicate the Italian naval threat hardened and its objective was carried out in spectacular fashion, off Cape Matapan, the most southerly point of Greece. On 27 March 1941, a British reconaissance plane spotted a large gathering

Above: **Italian cruisers *Fiume*, *Gorizia* and *Pola* undergoing manoeuvres.**

Left: **HMS *Revenge* sets sail from Malta in 1939, before the siege.**

of Italian ships. The squadron comprised eight cruisers, the prestige battleship Vittorio Veneto and a host of destroyers. Vittorio Veneto was the pride of the Italian fleet now her sister ship Littorio had been holed by the British at Taranto. Now she was poised with her support vessels to blow convoys destined for Greece out of the water.

Cunningham was instantly informed at his base in Alexandria. To back the aircraft sighting there were messages passed through the Italian secret service cipher which had been broken by the Allies. He

DAKAR DEBACLE

Among the military calamities faced by Britain in the first half of the war was the debacle of Dakar. British ships sailed to the colony of French West Africa with the aim of landing Free French Forces who would wrest control from the Vichy regime.

As they anchored off the main port of Dakar on 23 September 1940, General de Gaulle broadcast a series of messages to the colony's governor stating his intention to land troops. All of the messages were ignored. Five messengers sent ashore with similar news were likewise rebuffed.

De Gaulle began threatening to use force. In reply, the coastal guns and ships at anchor in the port let off a barrage at the British ships, preventing the planned landing. The next day the exchange of fire continued with the British battleship *Barham* being struck. Twenty four hours later the battleship *Resolution* was hit, this time sustaining more serious damage.

At this the British commanders and de Gaulle realised that their carefully laid plans to steal a march on Vichy France was quite literally being shot to pieces. Consequently, the ships pulled out of the engagement and returned humiliated to Freetown, the capital of Sierra Leone. Apart from the damage to its ships, the British also had to endure a reprisal air raid by the leaders of Vichy France directed against Gibraltar.

Below: **The big guns of the *Vittorio Veneto* unleash their fire power.**

grouped together three battleships, the aircraft carrier Formidable, four cruisers and as many destroyers as he could muster. If trouble was coming, the Royal Navy together with its Australian contingent were prepared.

Admiral Cunningham then made a move to protect the secrecy of the British activities which has since gone down as wartime folklore. A keen golfer, he played regularly in the same club in Alexandria as the Japanese consul who reported every move made by the British Mediterranean Fleet to its enemies. Not only did Cunningham take his clubs to play golf that afternoon but ostentatiously carried a suitcase, clearly bound for a night ashore. Having duped the tell-tale consul, he abandoned the case and slipped back aboard the battleship Warspite in time for an evening departure. Fortunately, the British ships did not pull out until after the Italians had carried out aerial reconnaissance of Alexandria harbour which revealed all were still at anchor. Italian Admiral Iachino was satisfied the British posed no danger.

The two forces, both travelling in independent groups, first clashed in the morning of 28 March. After 40 minutes of exchanging shells, neither side had scored a hit and the action was broken off. The British launched wave after wave of aircraft to pester the Italians who were themselves left virtually completely unprotected by their own air forces – which were stationed in easy range.

The British launched wave after wave of aircraft to pester the Italians

***Above: Vittorio Veneto* was the jewel in the Italian navy crown.**

Vittorio Veneto was hit by one torpedo but still managed to escape the ravages of the air bombardment. However the cruiser Pola was stopped in her tracks by British firepower. Iachino, who was without the benefit of radar and still apparently oblivious to the presence of British big ships, ordered two other cruisers to assist her. That night all three were attacked at short range. Two were quickly sunk without firing a shot. Pola and two other vessels were also sent to the bottom.

TIMED EXPLOSIVES

The British ships in the vicinity picked up 900 survivors before being scared off by the arrival of Luftwaffe planes. A further 270 men were plucked from the sea in the subsequent days but still the Italian casualties amounted to a devastating 2,400. The Battle of Matapan had been the biggest naval engagement of the war so far and dealt a serious blow to the Italian navy.

Vittorio Veneto was not to escape for long. A British submarine torpedoed her again in December 1941.

Despite the inferiority of Allied air cover, the Royal Navy continued to carry out admirable harrassing manoeuvres against the Italians and the Germans in the Mediterranean. Most notable were the contributions made by the cruisers Aurora and Penelope operating out of Malta who targeted convoys destined for Libya with immense success. Hitler and Mussolini were counting the cost of the contribution to the North African campaign made by the small island.

But the British didn't have it all their own way. When U-boats arrived in the Mediterranean, the fleet was deprived of the aircraft carrier Ark Royal which was sunk in November 1941, as well as the battleship Barham and two cruisers.

If the Italian navy was down, it certainly was not out as its attacks against British ships berthed in the harbour at Alexandria in December 1941 amply illustrated.

In the naval armoury were minute submarines, nick-named 'pigs' by their crew who were clad in frogmen's suits and sat astride the 22ft long craft. The 'pigs' were carried close to their position by regular submarines. Then it was the job of the crew to go in close to the target and attach timed explosives.

The Italians had made two abortive attempts using 'pigs' against the British during August and September 1940. This time there were to be no mistakes.

The Battle of Matapan dealt a serious blow to the Italian navy

After dark on 18 December an Italian submarine picked its way quietly and cautiously through mined seas to the approach of Alexandria harbour. There it off-loaded three 'pigs' and six crew, with a noiseless ripple on the water.

Now the Italian frogmen got to work. Beneath the waterline of the

Royal Navy battleship Queen Elizabeth, one team placed an explosive charge. Without being noticed, the two divers scrabbled ashore and posed as French sailors until they were seized by Egyptian police some time afterwards.

The second Italian team struggled to affix explosives to the side of a tanker. They were cold and stricken with sickness after spending too long underwater. But they didn't emerge from the water until their task had been completed. Egyptians arrested them as they attempted to pass the first control post of the harbour.

One member of the third team passed out but bobbed back to the surface and clutched a buoy until his partner finished the job in hand. The latter was having problems of his own, meanwhile, with a torn diving suit exposing him to lethal cold. Then the 'pig' plunged to the sea bed. Despite the growing effects of exposure, he dived to retrieve it, manhandled it 60 feet back to the base of his target, the Valiant, and set the detonator.

The men were still there when an explosion sent the ship lurching to portside

Above: **Probably the last photo taken of the Italian big ships before Matapan.**

He and his partner, now recovered, were picked up out of the water by a British motorboat and interrogated aboard Valiant. When they refused to speak about their operation, they were sent into the bowels of the ship close to where the charge was planted. The men were still there when an explosion sent the ship lurching to portside. They witnessed the effects of the blasts on the Queen Elizabeth and the tanker, too, with satisfaction. All the vessels would be

Below: Vittorio Veneto **smokes after attack by British Albacore planes.**

MALTESE CROSS

Malta was awarded the George Cross in April 1942 after four months of continuous bombardment by the Axis air forces. As the Royal Navy battled to get convoys containing vital supplies through to the island, they were hampered by U-boats and airborne attacks which wrecked merchant shipping. It wasn't until August 1942 that a convoy arrived intact. With the volley of bombs coming from the sky the people of Malta and the beleaguered defending forces were subject to the most appalling privations. Yet Malta was a key point in the Allied defences. Had it fallen into the hands of Germany, Rommel would probably have won the battle for North Africa and the outcome of the war might have been different.

out of action for some considerable time to come.

The Italian navy with Luftwaffe assistance continued to blockade Malta, the island which held the key to victory in North Africa. In December 1941 the Germans flew 169 bombing raids over Malta. In January 1942 the number rose to 262. Of course, the devastation took effect and Axis convoys began seeping through once more as Allied ships were put out of action, deprived themselves of fresh supplies. Nevertheless, Churchill was determined to keep Malta in Allied hands at all costs.

DAILY BOMBINGS

It wasn't until March 1942 that a British convoy managed to slip through the Italian net bringing in vital supplies. Attempts to get supplies to the island in June failed. Yet still the vicious air bombardment continued. Much of the island was laid waste by the daily bombings as Hitler and Mussolini plotted an invasion.

In answer to a pressing need for raw materials, the Allies planned a convoy of unprecedented size and strength in 'Operation Pedestal'. Setting off from Gibraltar to guard the supply ships were three aircraft carriers, two battleships, seven cruisers, 34 destroyers and eight submarines. The US carrier *Wasp* was also in evidence to bring new air forces to the island. The convoy departed on 10 August 1942 and came under repeated air attack. Both the Luftwaffe and Italy's Regia Aeronautica launched endless attacks with dive bombers, torpedo bombers and fighter aircraft.

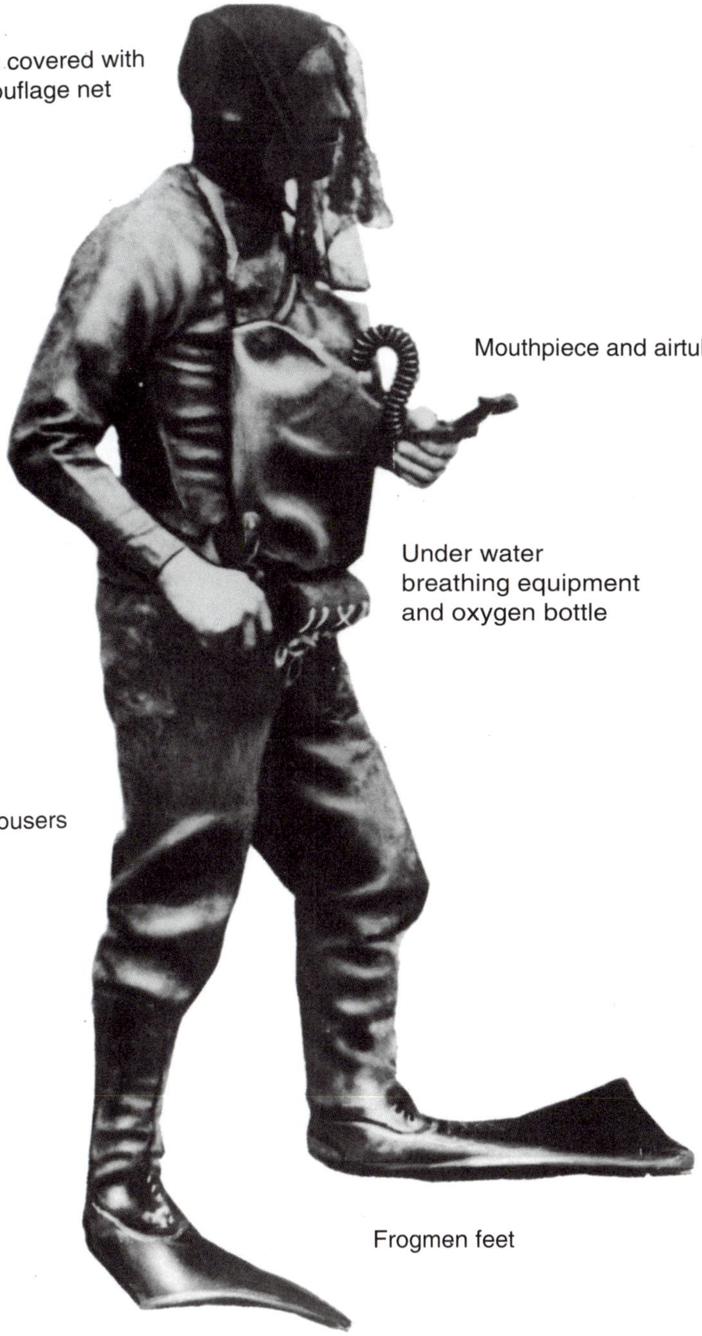

Churchill was determined to keep Malta in Allied hands at all costs

In the four day battle which pursued the convoy, the carrier *Eagle* was lost when it was sunk by U73, the cruisers *Cairo* and *Manchester* and the destroyer *Foresight* were sunk and ten out of the 15 merchant ships were floored. Many of the surviving escort ships were damaged. The Italian navy, denied air cover by its own airforce, refused to join the offensive and fell victim to a British submarine as it made its way back to port.

CRITICAL LOSSES

But even though the losses were critical, Malta was saved. Supplies that did filter through, amounting to some 30,000 tons, allowed the islanders and its battered forces to rebuild. It continued as a vital Allied base and deprived the Axis powers of a toehold which would have given them access to North Africa and the Middle East.

SINKING THE BISMARCK

Majestic and mighty, the brand new battleship which sailed under the swastika for the first time in May 1941 drew gasps of admiration from friend and foe alike.

The Bismarck cut an awesome sight as it sped through the waves. More than 800 feet long and almost 120 feet wide, it was heavy with armour plating and bristled with giant guns yet was still sleek and fast. Who could blame the proud Germans for believing it was unsinkable?

It was down to the Royal Navy to send the great ship to the ocean floor and it was an urgent task which they were eager to undertake. A powerful battleship like the Bismarck posed an enormous threat to the convoys bringing essential food and materials from across the Atlantic. Without this lifeline from America and Canada, Britain would have quickly been strangled.

Left: On the deck of the mighty *Bismarck*. **Below:** The battleship *Bismarck* undergoing sea trials.

Then suddenly there came a more pressing desire to see the Bismarck sunk. For on its maiden voyage it confronted HMS Hood, elegant queen of the Royal Navy, and sank it with the loss of almost all the crew. It was a devastating blow to navy pride and one which had to be avenged. The humblest sailor and the most powerful admiral in the British fleet felt to a man that Bismarck's maiden voyage must also be its last.

Bismarck was built in Hamburg long before the opening salvoes of World War II were fired. The vessel was launched amid great pomp and ceremony on 14 February 1939. Nazi top brass, including navy chief Raeder, Göring, Goebbels and Hess, joined Hitler on a lofty podium when the great hull rumbled down the slipway. There to christen the ship was Dorothea von Loewenfeld, granddaughter of the celebrated German chancellor Bismarck after whom the ship was named.

After World War I, the German navy had been stripped of virtually all its assets and the Treaty of Versailles had strictly forbidden the creation of military muscle like the Bismarck. Hitler had been rebuilding the fleet and Bismarck was the largest addition to date. It was officially listed at 35,000 tons, some 7,000 tons lighter than it actually was.

A powerful battleship like the Bismarck posed an enormous threat to the convoys

When war came, Bismarck stayed in dock while having chunky plating affixed to its sides and decks, the 22 sealed chambers beneath its waterline made watertight and the latest technology installed on the bridge. It was being fitted out for conflict to

become, as Germany's Admiral Tirpitz put it, 'an unsinkable gun platform'.

Its first taste of sea salt came when it left Hamburg on 15 September 1940 for trials in the shelter of Kiel Bay. There were teething troubles and Bismarck had to slink back to Hamburg for modifications. It wasn't until the following May that the ship was ready to set forth.

AIRCRAFT COVER

Hitler arrived at Gotenhafen (now Gdynia) for an inspection of his seaborne gem on 5 May, where Bismarck was patiently waiting to embark on its first trip. He was, it appears, kept unaware that its sailing date was imminent. The Führer, distrustful of his navy and its shortcomings, was wary of losing his prize vessel to the enemy and admiralty chiefs feared he would scupper their chances of getting underway at last.

Grand Admiral Erich Raeder believed it was vital to get Bismarck to sea. Germany now had the advantage of Atlantic ports in occupied France to provide bolt holes for its ships. Likewise, there was now extended aircraft cover from the Luftwaffe operating out of France. With summer drawing near, the lighter nights would significantly reduce the cover which was needed to spirit the ship into the Atlantic through the British sea blockade. Also, there was the increasing threat of America joining the war on the side of the Allies. The United States' naval power would dwarf that of Nazi Germany.

Fleet commander Gunther Lutjens was as confident in the strength of his new ship as the rest of Germany. But he had one nagging doubt that was shared by many senior officers in the Germany navy. It was the wisdom of going to sea without round-the-clock aircraft cover. In one sense, the Bismarck was out of date even before setting sail. The days of superships dominating the sea were rapidly diminishing. The sun was rising on the fleet air arms which

EYE WITNESS

Frank Hewlett joined the Royal Marines in 1939 when he was 20 years old.

'I was on HMS *Aurora*, an escort to the *Hood*. We followed her a day after she left Scapa Flow. When *Hood* was sunk we were 40 miles away. We saw a big flash on the horizon. When we heard the news, nobody believed it.

Then the *Prince of Wales* came within our sights. She was damaged and we escorted her back to Iceland. There was an unexploded shell inside her bows. If it had gone off it would have destroyed the ship. When the shell was removed, it was full of sand. It must have been sabotaged in Germany.

Afterwards, we went to Newfoundland and sank the supply ship *Max Albrecht*, sister ship to the *Altmark*. She went down with a U-boat still attached to her.'

In one sense, the Bismarck was out of date even before setting sail

Below: **HMS *Hood*, like the *Bismarck*, was thought by admirals to be invincible.**

Left: A confident crew parade aboard the *Bismarck* unaware of their fate.

could offer so much more by way of flexibility and accuracy. While both Japan and America were gearing up their navies for the new age, Germany and Britain were lagging behind, both caught unawares by the outbreak of war. The Bismarck had the capacity to hold just four float-planes, which were used primarily for reconnaissance missions.

Lutjens himself was the son of a retailer who shone at naval college in

It was only a matter of time before sighting of this monster was confirmed to London

Kiel after making an early resolution to combat any hurdle placed in front of him. A veteran of the sea assaults in World War I, he had already earned the distinction of a Knight's Cross during World War II through his courage in the Norwegian campaign of 1940.

Loyal to his country, 51-year-old Lutjens was nevertheless not a Nazi and refused to offer the party salute. Instead he preferred the time-honoured navy salute and wore the old fashioned insignia of the Kaiser's navy instead of a swastika.

On 19 May the Bismarck sailed under cover of darkness to begin 'Operation Rheinubung'. In the company of the 17,000-ton heavy cruiser Prinz Eugen, itself a formidable ship, the Bismarck purred off into the Baltic to be joined by other German navy vessels for its historic voyage. Its aim was to sink the battleships protecting convoys while the smaller Prinz Eugen picked off the merchantmen.

VULNERABILITY

Slipping down the Danish waterways and shadowing the Swedish coastline, it was only a matter of time before the sighting of this magnificent monster was confirmed to London. It was enough to spark Sir John Tovey, commander in chief of the Home Fleet, into action. At the pinnacle of his plan would be HMS Hood, 20 years old but still an inspiring sight. It was a match for the Bismarck in size and gunnery but its weakness lay in the relatively thin armour plating which covered its body and decks. It was this vulnerability that Bismarck exploited to the full.

On 22 May, just a day after news of the Bismarck arrived in London, Hood, the Prince of Wales and six other vessels set off from Scapa Flow. The following day two of the fleet, the Norfolk and the Suffolk, encountered the Bismarck in the Denmark Strait, between Iceland and Greenland. As they dashed for cover in the icy fog, the Bismarck registered their presence and fired off a warning shot.

DEADLY BLOW

The mood was tense among officers and men on the Hood and the Prince of Wales as the hunt for their fearsome quarry continued. All the crew were poised to strike but lost their chance when their ships slipped past the giant battleship in the darkness as it skirted the Greenland ice pack.

Bismarck continued altering its course, not greatly but enough to put the ships commanded by Vice-Admiral Lancelot Holland in a

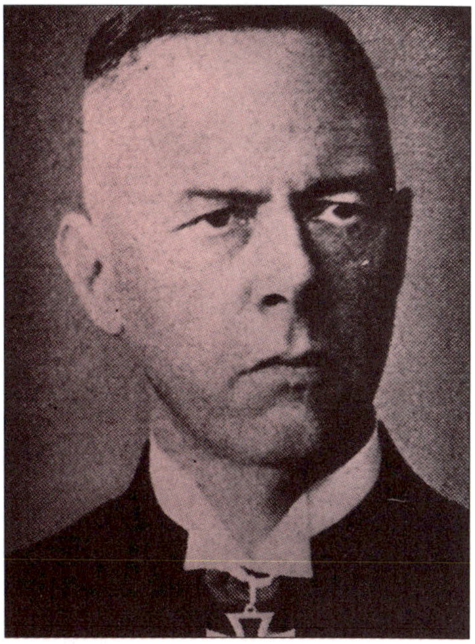

Above: Following his encounter with *Hood*, Admiral Lutjens bolted for France.

HUNTING THE *BISMARCK*

On 19 May the *Bismarck* sailed under cover of darkness to begin Operation Rheinubung. In the company of the heavy cruiser *Prinz Eugen*, *Bismarck* headed through the Skagerrak to the Norwegian coast. Passing so close to the Danish and Swedish coasts, it was only a matter of time before the two warships were sighted by British agents, and the news transmitted to London. Sir John Tovey was ordered to get the *Bismarck*.

On 22 May, just a day after news of the *Bismarck* arrived in London, the largest ship in the Royal Navy, HMS *Hood*, and the brand-new battleship HMS *Prince of Wales* set off from Scapa Flow in the Orkneys, accompanied by six other vessels.

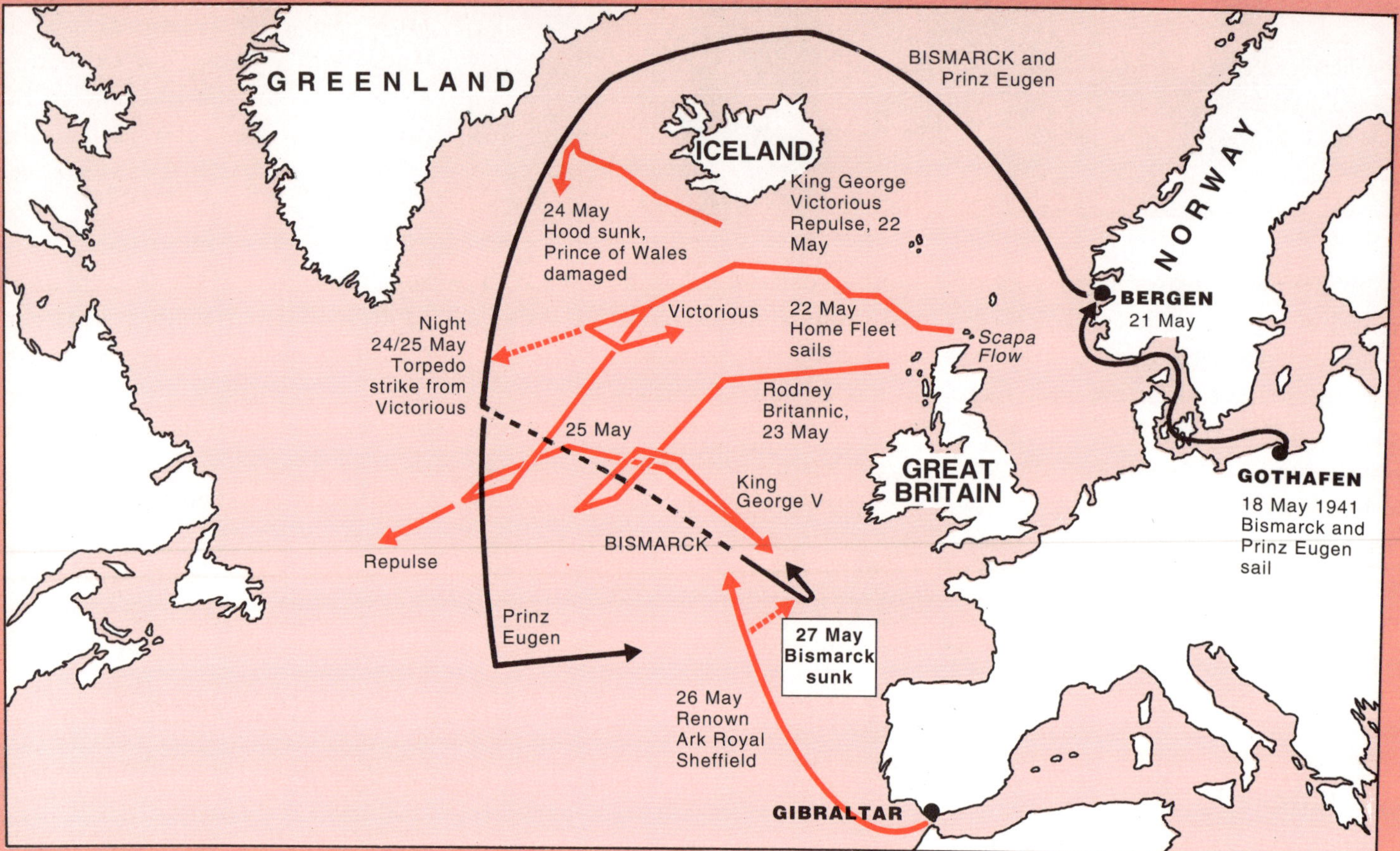

quandary. The initial plan had been to creep up on the *Bismarck* under cover of darkness in a short range strike. Now the *Hood* was forced to make a broad sweep at the enemy and would be exposed to the brunt of its firepower.

When they sighted *Bismarck*, the *Hood* and *Prince of Wales*, travelling in close formation, were about 17 miles distant. At Admiral Holland's command, both ships began a charge at the enemy.

Lutjens was under orders to engage only the escorts of convoys. He wasn't looking for a duel and had hoped to avoid one. But now he had no choice. When the *Hood* and *Prince of Wales* closed the gap to 13 miles, they fired. Seconds later, the *Bismarck* and the *Prinz Eugen* replied in kind. And while the British ships failed to find their targets, the Germans had them well and truly in range.

> ***The initial plan had been to creep up on the Bismarck under cover of darkness***

The second salvo from *Prinz Eugen*'s guns struck the *Hood*, igniting anti-aircraft ammunition. Another hit and then a third slaughtered many of the gun crews taking shelter. Still the guns from both sides continued firing.

It was during a manouevre by the *Hood* trying for a better angle that the deadly blow was delivered by the *Bismarck*. A shell plunged down into the heart of the ship, penetrating the

***Above: Prinz Eugen* was released from escort duty to escape the Royal Navy.**

deck with apparent ease. Somewhere in the bowels, it silently sparked an ammunition store, maybe two. The effect was catastrophic. Observers from both sides were astonished to see a massive plume of fire and smoke burst from the middle of the ship when there had been no explosion. The Hood, the most prestigious

The Hood folded in two and plunged to the bottom of the sea

ship in old England, folded in two and plunged to the bottom of the sea.

With it went the vast majority of the 1,400 crew, trapped in the wreckage. It was several hours before a British cruiser came hunting for survivors. It found only three, cold and near death, clinging to small rafts in the middle of an oil slick.

The Prince of Wales was soon reeling from the effect of shells. It had been hit seven times, lost two officers and 11 men and was plagued with difficulties in its gunnery, making its own attack ineffective. Moments after its stunned crew saw the Hood ditching into the sea, it was decided to withdraw. The showdown had lasted just 21 minutes.

Britain was devastated by the loss of the Hood and its men. After the shock, the public were baying for revenge – or feared the Bismarck really was indestructible. There was no time for sentimentality among the naval officers now in hot pursuit of the Bismarck.

The battleship Prince of Wales, plus the cruisers Norfolk and Suffolk shadowed the Bismarck as it moved south. Admiral Tovey, aboard King George V, was in command of Victorious, Repulse, four cruisers and nine destroyers hoping to intercept Bismarck from the south.

Visibility was poor, however, and the radar used by Suffolk to track its movements was patchy. Bismarck had, in fact, not escaped unscathed. It was holed twice by British shells which forced it to reduce speed and lost the vessel valuable fuel.

BISMARCK HURT

Lutjens felt he had no choice but to head for France for repairs. He released the Prinz Eugen to make a clean getaway, firing lazily at the Prince of Wales by way of distraction. Then he set a course which he hoped would take him to friendly France or within the torpedo range of a protective U-boat.

It was with some degree of surprise that he and his crew looked up to the skies some hours later and saw a group of circus-style planes buzzing towards them. These were the Swordfish planes which had set off from the Victorious in order to wreak havoc on the Bismarck. With

***Below:* Hitler failed to share the nation's pride in the navy.**

◆ EYE WITNESS ◆

Able Seaman Robert Kilburn was one of the three who survived the sinking of the *Hood*.

I was a member of the anti-aircraft gun crew but, of course, we weren't needed. There were only two other people with me at the time. The others were in a shelter deck – a shell had gone in there and killed all of them, about 200 men – but I didn't know that at the time.

One of the shells hit one of the ready-fuse lockers for the four inch guns and there was a fire on board the upper deck and the ammunition was exploding. We were laid on the deck and then there was this terrific explosion. It was most peculiar, the dead silence that followed it – I don't know if we were deaf.

One of the other men was dead and the other one had his sides cut open and all his innards were tumbling out. I went to the ship's side to be sick. I noticed that the ship was rolling over and the bows were coming out of the water so I started taking off my tin hat, gas mask, anti-flash gear, overcoat, oilskin, so that I would have a chance to swim. With the ship rolling over, I just went into the water and the water came up to me.

I was terrified. I had a small rubber life belt on which you blew up – it was partially blown up. I started swimming away from the ship. I had a right belt on so I took my knife off and cut the belt off to breathe better. The ship rolled over and the yard arms which had been broken during the action hit me across the legs and the wireless aerials tangled around my legs, pulling me down with the ship. I cut my seaboots off with the knife and shot up, like a cork out of a bottle. I must have been about 10 ft down by then. The ship was around 10 yards away from me with her bows straight up in the air – and she just sank.

In 1989 a team led by Dr Robert Ballard located the crusted hulk of the *Bismarck* (above) nestling on the ocean floor. Dr Ballard, the man who found and photographed the wreck of the *Titanic*, was aboard the *Star Hercules* when he discovered the *Bismarck* three miles beneath the ocean during a 10-day expedition. Among the photographs he took with a remote controlled underwater camera were those of discarded boots, the teak deck which was still intact and a 14-inch gun with a sea anenome bursting from its barrel.

their single propellers and stacked wings they look like something from a different age. Nevertheless, the torpedo they carried beneath their fuselage was powerful enough to reckon with. The brave pilots of the Swordfish planes flew in low despite the barrage of anti-aircraft fire. Just one torpedo hit the mark. Yet all the eight attacking Swordfish planes survived the hair-raising attack and landed safely back on Victorious in the dark with next to no fuel.

The damage sustained by Bismarck was enough to make Lutjens review his course. With masterly intuition he turned suddenly westwards and, in doing so, shook off the Royal Navy shadow. It took 31 hours for the British to locate the Bismarck again.

By now most of the British ships in reach had been called in to help. Yet due to a series of mishaps and misunderstandings, they were unable to find the roaming battleship, having turned in the wrong direction. In addition, many were running short of fuel and had to splinter from the body of the fleet to find more. Navy top brass was becoming increasingly nervous. Unaware that the Bismarck had been wounded, they knew its path must be taking it towards the 11 Allied convoys presently crossing the Atlantic.

On 26 May intrepid Swordfish planes found* Bismarck *again and attacked

On 26 May intrepid Swordfish, this time from the Ark Royal, found Bismarck again and attacked. Two torpedoes struck the big ship, wrecking the steering gear and ruining a propeller. It meant that Bismarck not only had to slow down further but also became locked on to a course which brought it directly into the path of the opposition, thanks to the jammed rudder.

The following day Bismarck came within range of the battleships Rodney and King George V. They weren't alone and soon the Bismarck was surrounded by British ships

Above: **The *Prince of Wales* was one of many ships to hunt the *Bismarck*.**

firing when they could. Bismarck took punch after punch, losing men and guns with every minute of the merciless onslaught. Fires raged fore and aft while ammunition exploded all around. Yet still it stayed afloat.

Afterwards, British sailors admitted they felt little elation at seeing the enemy ship battered so badly. However, they had no option but to continue the barrage while the Bismarck still fired back.

HITLER'S OUTRAGE

When streams of German sailors plunged into the sea, the shelling stopped. Tovey was not only mindful of their safety but also that of his own men. Fuel and ammunition were running desperately low in his fleet. It would not be long before the lurking U-boats would turn up looking for easy pickings.

Satisfied the Bismarck would no longer menace the shipping lanes of the Atlantic, he gave orders for the British ships to withdraw. The only ship left with torpedoes, the Dorsetshire, remained to finish off the job. Controversy raged afterwards whether it was a British torpedo or a German sailor who sank the Bismarck by opening the sea-cocks.

The situation for the men floundering in the water after leaping from the Bismarck was bleak. At first the Dorsetshire and the destroyer Maori hauled up survivors. But their goodwill came to an abrupt end following the reported sighting of a U-boat. The ships revved up and pulled away from the bobbing survivors, ignoring their cries for help and leaving them to suffer a lingering death in the waves. Two other vessels rescued a handful of survivors between them. Only 115 of the crew escaped with their lives out of a total of 2,206.

When news of the sinking reached Hitler he was outraged. Never mind that a fleet of five battleships, three battle cruisers, two aircraft carriers, 13 cruisers, 33 destroyers and eight submarines had been involved in the execution. He bitterly regretted ever putting his classic ship to sea.

Below: **How the incredible story of pursuit was told to the British public.**

ABOVE THE HEADLINES ... comes extra good news There's no change in the quality of BROWN & POLSON CORNFLOUR AND CUSTARD

News Chronicle

Imperial

No. 29,858 WEDNESDAY, MAY 28, 1941 RADIO PAGE 2 ONE PENNY

BISMARCK: THE FIRST FULL STORY

Air and Sea Chase Lasted Four Days, Covered 1,750 Miles

CANADIAN PLANES CAME FROM NEWFOUNDLAND | A FLEET SAILED UP FROM GIBRALTAR

FROM THE ADMIRALTY AND THE AIR MINISTRY THERE CAME LAST NIGHT THE FIRST FULL ACCOUNT OF THE FOUR DAYS OF ATLANTIC BATTLE AND PURSUIT WHICH CULMINATED AT 11.1 A.M. YESTERDAY IN THE SINKING OF THE BISMARCK, FINEST FIGHTING SHIP IN HITLER'S FLEET.

The 35,000-ton Nazi warship was hunted for more than 1,750 miles before she was sunk by torpedoes from the cruiser Dorsetshire about 400 miles west of Brest.

The main body of the Home Fleet, under Admiral J. C. Tovey aboard the battleship King George V., a force from Gibraltar under Vice-Admiral Sir James Somerville, in the Renown, and the battleships Rodney and Ramillies, all answered the call: "Get the Bismarck."

These naval forces consisted of at least four battleships, two battle cruisers, two aircraft-carriers, four cruisers and a number of destroyers led by the famous Cossack.

In addition, machines of the Canadian Air Force came out from Newfoundland to search, Coastal Command planes shadowed the quarry on the chase, while from the Ark Royal and the Victorious Fleet Air Arm planes swept the skies reporting every twist and turn of the Bismarck as she tried desperately to break through the gigantic net.

The Bismarck's attendant cruiser, the Prinz Eugen, vanished during the chase, but yesterday Mr. Churchill said "measures are being taken in respect of her."

Apart from the Hood, blown up when the German ship was first brought to action after leaving Bergen, the Prince of Wales, one of Britain's newest battleships, is the only vessel of the Fleet to suffer damage.

This is the Admiralty communiqué:

Air reconnaissance by Coastal Command aircraft revealed that a German battleship and cruiser, which they had previously located in the Norwegian port of Bergen, had sailed.

Churchill Gives News From Bits Of Paper

TANTALISING

NEXT TWO DAYS ARE VITAL IN BATTLE FOR CRETE

From BERTHA GASTER

CAIRO, Tuesday.

THE BATTLE FOR CRETE HAS NARROWED DOWN TO AN INTENSE STRUGGLE BETWEEN CONCENTRATED GERMAN FORCES AND ALLIED LINES ALONG THE FEW MILES OF COASTLINE SEPARATING MALEME FROM THE TOWN OF CANEA.

The decisive phase of the campaign is being fought out among the olive fields and groves west of Canea, where the German troops, supported by the same cover of intensive bombing as was used yesterday, made renewed attacks on our lines last night, pushing through the breach made earlier and forcing our troops to withdraw from the original line of defences to the rear.

Australians, New Zealanders and British troops still guard the line of approach to the town, which is not captured.

The next two days will probably be vital in this island fight.

"The situation is serious."

Crete

1,000 Saved from Ships Lost In Battle of Crete

ON PAGE TWO

Greatest Sea v. Air Battle in History. By One Who Was There.

The End of the Bismarck. By Maj. Fielding Eliot

ROOSEVELT SPEAKS

ARCTIC CONVOYS

Manning a ship on one of the treacherous Arctic convoys was perhaps the bleakest role in the whole war. For on these storm-lashed northern routes the weather collaborated with the enemy to make each day more miserable than the last.

Arctic convoys began after Soviet Russia was invaded by Germany and became an eminent ally of Great Britain. It wasn't a matter of survival to Britain as in the case of the Atlantic convoys.

Above: **A U-boat crew operating in northern waters survey their iced-up weapons.**

Here was an excrcise designed to appease Russia's leader Stalin. To exploit the opportunities for trade between the two countries, ships had to travel in the vicinity of the north pole where, for winter weeks on end, the sun never rose.

Hidden dangers under the waves included icebergs as well as U-boats. In the air the threat lay in frostbite alongside the dive-bombing planes of the Luftwaffe. The iron-grey steel hulls belonging to the powerful surface ships of the German navy were often masked by soupy fogs or dense blizzards.

REGULAR LOSSES

The sailors aboard knew they were being hunted. The buzz of a German reconnaissance plane overhead was a sure indication that an attack was being prepared. Sometimes, not often enough, the convoy skirted the edge of the polar ice and slid through the ocean without being noticed. Sole reward for the hapless mariners was the chance of arriving in one piece at their destination.

Ships carrying the precious cargoes travelled under protection of British and American warships in convoys, usually between Scotland or Iceland and Murmansk, Russia. These northern waters were particularly risky. After Germany invaded Norway, it meant there were ports and airfields accessible to German forces within easy range. Hitler was also dedicated

Hidden underwater dangers included icebergs and U-boats

to victory over Russia. The sea battles to stop the convoys getting through to Stalin assumed greater importance given the personal interest of the Führer.

In reply the Allies did have the benefit of technology. Their grasp of the German naval secret codes was now accomplished. Yet despite rerouting to evade the attentions of the Arctic U-boats, convoys were still

Far left: **A British convoy leaves the warmth of British waters for Russia.**
Left: **Two Valentine tanks included in the aid sent to Russia.**

suffering regular losses. Virtually every convoy which set sail between March and June 1942 was attacked, either by U-boat or by the Luftwaffe. In all, 21 ships were lost in addition to the cruisers Edinburgh and Trinidad. Those losses were balanced against the safe arrival of 124 ships.

Now it seemed Germany was ready to pitch its prestige big ships into the fray. Britain's Admiralty was nervous. Knowing that ships like the Admiral

Virtually every convoy which set sail between March and June 1944 was attacked

Hipper and Admiral Scheer were in northern waters, biding their time in safe ports, made the prospects for any future convoys seem gloomy. Also there was Lützow formerly known as Deutschland. (Hitler changed the name because the sinking of a ship called 'Germany' would cause depression at home and would be the butt of jokes among his enemies.) Worst of all

◆ EYE WITNESS ◆

Forbes Brown, from Victoria, British Columbia, joined the Royal Canadian Navy in 1941 and trained as an Asdic operator.

"My first trip was in a corvette, HMCS *Algoma*, across the North Atlantic as a convoy escort. With Asdic we transmitted a sound beam and it reflected back if there was a submarine under the water. I could hardly believe it when I picked up a contact. Action stations were sounded. It was about 600 yards ahead. About 40 depth charges were dropped.

Following the last one there was a tremendous explosion underwater. It blew out all the safety valves on the engine and there were blue flames shooting off the deck. We suspected the last charge hit a torpedo head. Still there were plenty of other U-boats about. We started off with 62 ships in the convoy and ended up with 41. It was hairy. After that trip we were supplied with sheepskins so we suspected we were going north. As usual, it was a foul up. We were off to the Mediterranean."

was the presence of the huge battleship Tirpitz, sister ship of the Bismarck and the pride of the German fleet, with awesome firepower and astonishing capabilities.

Code-crackers revealed the large boats were preparing to depart and do battle. Convoy PQ17, sailing out of Iceland's capital, Reykjavik, on 27 June, comprised 33 ships and a tanker with an escort of six destroyers, four corvettes, two submarines and two anti-aircraft ships It was in danger of a severe mauling.

Left: **Some of the British and US ships involved in safeguarding the Arctic convoy routes.**

In London, it was clear that the enemy could pounce at any time. At sea, the convoy captains were equally expectant, wondering where and when the ferocious strike would come. Each bank of fog came as a welcome relief as the convoy made its way steadily northwards.

Information now coming out of the cipher service indicated the big ships were setting out from their base. It was enough for Sir Dudley Pound, First Lord of the Admiralty, to order the convoy ships to scatter for their best protection. Little did he know that Hitler himself had intervened in the operation. He barred the use of valuable, prestige ships like the Tirpitz unless complete safety could be guaranteed. That meant British and American aircraft carriers were safely out of range.

Tirpitz was not heading for the convoy. The information from the secret message service had been misconstrued – with devastating results. As ordered, the convoy scattered. Armed ships pulled away from the merchant ships to search for the Tirpitz and its team. Apprehensively, the watch officers scanned the horizon, expecting to see the massive vessel looming. Nothing appeared. Now their nagging anxieties lay with the fate of the ships they had left behind, with good cause. Twenty of Convoy PQ17's vessels were lost when the U-boats and the Luftwaffe seized the golden opportunity.

Watch officers scanned the horizon, expecting to see the massive vessel looming

In fact, the Tirpitz did sail on 5 July but was recalled following the success the attack had already achieved. Neither did the big ships take part in action against the subsequent convoy, PQ18. Hitler once again erred on the side of caution rather than risk another humiliating loss at sea to parallel the Bismarck. Before reaching safety, PQ18 lost ten ships to aircraft and three to U-boats. The escort ships which this time stayed close to their charges, claimed a number of planes with anti-aircraft fire and Allied fighter aircraft while one U-boat was sunk.

When the might of the German navy next put to sea it was at the end of the year following some intensive exercises. Their target was a 14-ship convoy, JW51B, which set out from Scotland destined for Kola on 22

Below: Scharnhorst was the scourge of convoys in northern waters.

Left: **RAF Mosquitos pounced on surfaced submarines and enemy shipping at every opportunity and soon helped to tip the balance of the battle.**

December. It was the second leg of a convoy, the first of which had crossed the sea without being spotted. A flotilla of destroyers joined up with the convoy on Christmas Day. Sailing to meet them were the cruisers which had accompanied the first part of the convoy.

The weather was poor, hampering visibility and identification of ships

This time, the code-breakers let down the protection ships by failing to translate a vital enemy message in good time. Admiral Hipper and the pocket battleship Lützow, in the company of six destroyers, put to sea on 30 December. The British had no idea of the threat in the absence of deciphered enemy messages.

The weather was poor, hampering visibility and therefore the identification of ships whose shadows suddenly appeared in the mist. The first the Allied destroyers knew of the imminent danger was when the destroyer Obdurate was fired on by one of the German destroyers.

While the convoy pulled back under the cover of a smoke screen, the destroyers set about repelling the advance. Four times the Hipper tried to break through to fire on the convoy and on each occasion the destroyers pushed it back. The only damage Admiral Hipper did was on the last attack when an eight inch shell ploughed into the Onslow. One other destroyer, Achates, was sunk along with the minesweeper Bramble before the Battle of the Barents Sea was over.

GERMAN DEFEAT

Hipper was forced to retire into a snow storm when it was hit three times. Lützow, although in a prime position to attack the convoy, kept its guns silent. A German destroyer which suddenly emerged from a snowstorm close to the Sheffield, by now pursuing Hipper, was soon sunk. The convoy continued on its way.

A squally, inconclusive battle, it was nevertheless a humiliating defeat for the German navy. One of its prestige ships was forced to pull away with substantial damage while

◆ EYE WITNESS ◆

Raymond Lund, who joined the Royal Navy in 1942 when he was 17, accompanied nine Arctic convoys on the destroyer *Scorpion*.

‘We were never dry. And if ever you went to change your clothes you had to do it very quickly as you never knew when ‘action stations’ would be called. We were often at action stations 22 hours a day.

There wasn't much sleep for anyone. When I did sleep it was fully clothed on a bench with my arms wrapped around a pillar on the mess deck. I even slept standing up.

About 16 to 18 U-boats would form a line ahead of us. We used to charge through and disperse them. In the summer it was never dark, in the winter it was never light. We used to like a bit of a rough sea. It may have been uncomfortable but it kept the U-boats away.

When it was cold, it was difficult to breathe. I used to pull something wollen across my mouth to break the rush of air as it came through. Never at any time could we touch metal. It would burn and stick to your fingers and it would mean a trip to the sick bay. In the middle of winter we weren't allowed on the upper deck where the temperature could be as low as minus 50 degrees C.

The most memorable day of the war for me was when we sank the *Scharnhorst*. It was Boxing Day 1943. We were escorting a convoy to Russia when we had news that she was at sea. We were soon given orders to leave the convoy and proceeded to intercept.

The *Duke of York* came up behind. There were two destroyers to her starboard and two to port. The *Scorpion* fired torpedoes at the *Scharnhorst* which slowed her up. Her guns were firing all the time as well. We saw various hits. Then an Arctic fret obscured our view. We knew by a terrific explosion when she had gone. Our ship picked up over 30 survivors. We took them back to Scapa Flow and they became prisoners of war.’

the aim of the attack, the sinking of the convoy, was frustrated.

Hitler was furious at the debacle. On New Year's Day 1943 he threatened to decommission the German fleet completely and break up the big ships for scrap. Grand Admiral Raeder, he claimed, lacked the pioneering spirit of adventure that was necessary to win wars. Raeder responded immediately, by asking to be relieved of his command.

DARING PLAN

In his place came Admiral Karl Dönitz, hitherto commander of the U-boat service. Hitler much preferred Dönitz to his predecessor and, in turn, Dönitz was able to convince the Führer of the need to maintain the surface fleet. Nevertheless, he too was unable to find further successes, despite his efforts.

The British Admiralty chiefs appeared to have a greater faith in the destructive power of the German fleet than Hitler himself. In northern waters, they remained wary of the threat posed by Tirpitz, Lützow and Scharnhorst. Indeed, Arctic convoys were even cancelled on the basis that the big three might sail.

By September 1943 a daring plan had been drawn up to rid the convoys of the naval menace once and for all. The aim was for four-man midget submarines armed with two one-ton charges to creep into the Norwegian anchorage at Altenfjord and place crippling explosives on the undersides of Scharnhorst, Lützow and Tirpitz. In utmost secrecy, the mission began with full-sized submarines towing the midgets to the mouth of the fjord.

Unluckily, Scharnhorst was at sea for trials when the six midget submarines went into action. The tiny undersea craft assigned to blow up Lützow was lost as it made its way there. Another lost its tow and was forced to jettison the charges. A third caught fire and had to turn back. But the success of submarines X5, X6 and X7 more than made up for the disappointing performances of the other three.

When one of the midgets was spotted the alarm was raised. One was forced to surrender. The other sank with the loss of two lives and the third was sunk, although it is not known when and how. But all this unfolded after at least three of the charges had been laid. Although held captive on the ship itself, the seamen

Hitler threatened to decommission the German fleet completely

Below: **An X-craft, like those used against *Tirpitz*, with its commander on deck.**

Right: **X-craft crew got fresh air whenever they could to relieve the closet-style condition of their vessel.**

who surrendered refused to reveal the whereabouts of the explosives. Finally, the Germans got their answer when the mighty Tirpitz was lifted five feet out of the water. It would take seven months to complete repairs. Both surviving submarine commanders, Lieutenants Donald Cameron and Godfrey Place, were rewarded after the war with the VC.

POOR WEATHER

Lützow abandoned the hunt for the Arctic convoys soon afterwards, returning to occupied Poland for operations in the Baltic. That left the last remaining danger – Scharnhorst – in Norwegian waters, fully equipped and ready for action. It was only a matter of time before she would venture forth to take on a convoy and this troubled the British commanders whose job it was to protect the merchant ships.

On Christmas Day 1943 the order to sail finally came for the expectant Scharnhorst crew, eager as they were to salvage the good name of the German navy. The ship emerged from its protective fjord in the company of five destroyers that evening in search of convoy JW55B.

> **Scharnhorst *had no idea it was heading towards the Royal Navy's big cruisers***

Poor weather once again played its part, this time to the advantage of the Allies. Scharnhorst hived away from its destroyer escorts. Lacking the superior intelligence assistance open to the Allies, it had no idea it was heading towards some of the Royal Navy's big cruisers in the region.

First to fire on the German was HMS Belfast who picked up the enemy by radar. Norfolk then joined the battle by opening fire and scoring a hit. The British ships broke off their action, not wanting to scare Scharnhorst back into port.

Next to spy it was Sheffield some two hours later. In the spat that followed it was Norfolk's turn to sustain damage. Yet the British cruisers did a brilliant job. They drove the unsuspecting Scharnhorst into the arms of Admiral Fraser on the Duke of York. At a range of 1,200 yards, the Duke of York opened fire with its devastating 14-inch guns. This time Scharnhorst fled to the east, making good ground against its pursuers. But critical damage forced the German ship to steady its speed. It gave

British destroyers ample opportunity to unleash some torpedoes, finally sinking the Scharnhorst at 7.45pm. Just 36 survivors were saved from a crew of 2,000.

Tirpitz was now the lonc operator in the Arctic. Although it rarely saw action, its presence alone was sufficient cause to divert air and naval craft from other duties. It would not be allowed to escape unscathed for long. Nevertheless, it was to be aircraft that delivered the deathblows to this massive battlewagon.

TIRPITZ SUNK

The first sortie against it began from Scapa Flow on 30 March 1944 with the Duke of York, Belfast, Anson and the aircraft carrier Victorious in 'Operation Tungsten'. On 3 April, 42 Barracuda aircraft loaded with powerful, armour-piercing bombs set off after their quarry, which was at that moment in Norway's Altenfjord, preparing to go to sea.

LEND-LEASE

Still hoping to keep his country out of war, President Roosevelt steered the Lend-Lease Act through Congress in March 1941. It gave the President powers to send military and material aid to countries at war with Germany and Italy with the sole provision being that they repay the loans at the end of the war. Although it was opposed fiercely by some factions, the Act had the beneficial effect of boosting the American defence industry even before the country went to war with Japan.

Above: **Wintry seas kept British sailors perpetually wet.** ***Left:*** **Proud gunners on HMS** ***Duke of York*** **posed for the camera in front of their guns after sinking the German battlecruiser** ***Scharnhorst*****.**

The action devastated the upper decks of Tirpitz and killed 122 men. Yet the supership stayed afloat, to the disappointment of the Allies.

Several other bids to sink the ship by Fleet Air Arm aircraft were thwarted by poor weather while still more failed to deliver the necessary punch to put it out of action. Aircraft were being lost in these vain attempts, forcing the Admiralty to think again. They called in the assistance of Bomber Command which had vast 'Tallboy' bombs.

Taking off from a Russian base on 15 September 1944, a cloud of Lancaster bombers rained 16 such bombs on the Tirpitz, causing extensive damage. This time it would take nine months to make the repairs.

If the crippled Tirpitz had not moved to Tromsö that October, the Allies might have been satisfied. Germany wanted it as a floating gun platform to defend an expected invasion in the region by the Allies. Yet the Admiralty was disturbed by the ship's sudden activity and feared new attacks at sea.

On 29 October, 32 Lancaster bombers in 'Operation Obviate' caused more devastation. However it wasn't until 'Operation Catechism' got underway involving the men and Lancaster aircraft of 617 Squadron – 'the Dambusters' – on 12 November 1944 that Tirpitz finally rolled over and died. About 1,000 crewmen were lost, trapped inside the great ship as it turned turtle.

CORAL SEA AND MIDWAY

Pearl Harbor may have been the most spectacular action undertaken by the Japanese navy but it wasn't the last.

Here was the world's third most powerful navy staffed by efficient, skilled commanders and loyal sailors. It was their brief to roam the seas around Japan's newly acquired territories, protecting land-based flanks by fending off attacks from air and sea.

The Japanese navy played a major role in the domino fall of Asian and Pacific lands and islands, including that of Thailand, Hong Kong, the Philippines and Burma. Indeed, the noose put around Singapore by the Japanese navy during February 1942 ensured that none of the defending British or Australian troops could escape by sea and all those who survived the fighting were consequently taken prisoner.

When the Japanese cast their eyes in the direction of Java, the jewel they wanted in their crown, an allied naval force squared up to the challenge. Under Dutch officer Admiral Karel Doorman, a fleet of heavy and light cruisers and destroyers gathered from the Dutch, American, British and Australian navies determined to keep the Japanese out of the oil-rich colony.

BATTLE OF JAVA

The Battle of the Java Sea began on 27 February and was one of the largest naval confrontations the world had seen since World War I.

Both sides seemed equally matched when they began a mutual bombardment with guns. But the Japanese wreaked havoc when they edged closer to the Allied fleet and opened up with torpedoes.

Hostilities ceased while the Allied ships refuelled only to resume within hours beneath the moonlight. Doorman was delighted when he once again encountered the Japanese and sought to end their plans to invade Java once and for all. Little did he realise that he was being snapped up in a tactical pincer. When

The Japanese wreaked havoc when they edged closer to the Allied fleet

Left: **Crews from USS *Lexington* go into action in the Coral Sea in May 1942.**
Below: **Carrying the wounded off USS *Marblehead* in Netherlands East docks after the Battle of Java in February 1942.**

more torpedoes blasted his force in a surprise attack from a second angle there was chaos. In just seven hours, five Allied warships were sunk, while only one Japanese destroyer sustained damage. Doorman himself was lost when his cruiser De Ruyter went down.

BATTLE OF MIDWAY

So far the Emperor's fleet remained virtually unscathed by the ravages of war. During all its activities in the sea-borne invasions of Pacific and South East Asian islands only a total of four destroyers had been put out of action. Meanwhile, only four US destroyers had escaped to Australia from the treacherous waters around the Dutch East Indies. It seemed as if the Japanese navy was invincible.

At the time the US felt confident enough only to take pot shots at the Japanese. The first skirmish took place in January when two US task forces bombed Japanese bases on the Marshalls and Gilberts. It was a tame event but nevertheless proved a small boost for American morale, being the first strike back at the enemy.

In March US planes took off from the carriers Yorktown and Lexington to attack two ports on Papua New Guinea which had just been overrun by the Japanese. Again, the results were negligible.

America determinedly began to gather its strength. US troops were sent to Darwin in Australia and were

The US felt confident enough only to take pot shots at the Japanese

by February under the command of General Douglas MacArthur. In fact, almost four times as many troops were sent from America to the Pacific at the time than took the shorter hop across the Atlantic to reinforce the Allied armies aiming to defeat Hitler.

Australian divisions, too, were recalled from the Middle East to help defend their homeland.

And the tide of Japanese successes was set to ebb as early as May 1942 with two historic seaborne clashes between Japan and America, one in

Above, right, far right: **The triumphant Doolittle raid on Tokyo. A B-25 comes under starter's orders on its way to Japan. Doolittle is pictured later by his crashed aircraft in China.**

◆ BATTLE OF MIDWAY

Japan wanted a base within striking range of Hawaii. It also wanted the US fleet destroyed. Yamamoto hatched a plan to secure such a base and lure the US Navy to its downfall in the process. He launched a diversionary attack on the Aleutians while he struck at Midway Island. Unfortunately for him the Americans knew he was coming and had put to sea. The first wave of Japanese bombers caught many US aircraft on the ground at Midway. Nevertheless, enough got airborne to make a second Japanese strike necessary. It was while the Japanese were rearming that US Admiral Spruance struck. Aircraft from *Yorktown* and *Enterprise* destroyed four Japanese carriers; on the US side, *Yorktown* was sunk.

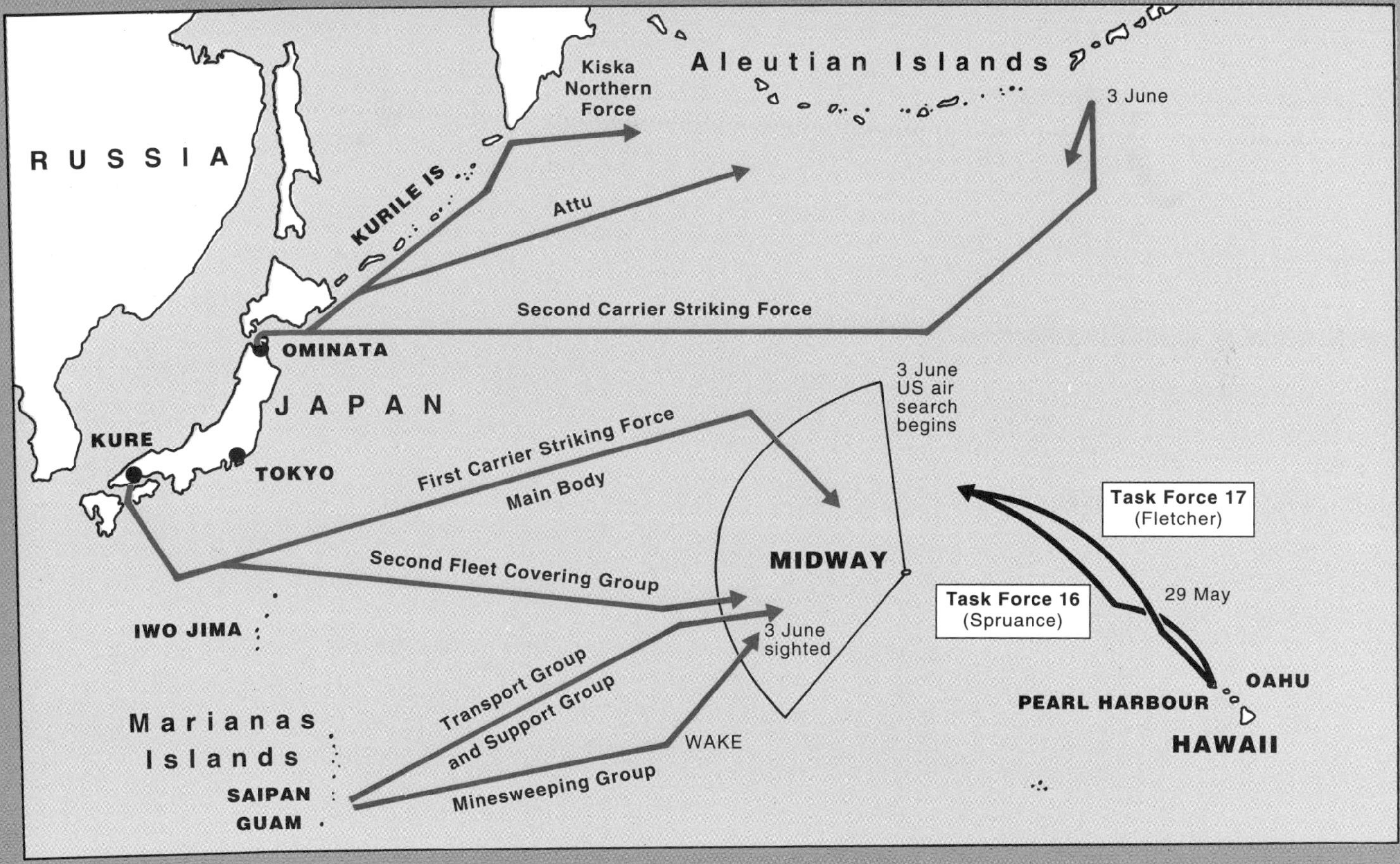

the Coral Sea and the other around the island of Midway.

The Battle of the Coral Sea was not notable for its end result as the outcome was so murky it was difficult to distinguish a winner. Japan certainly wasn't defeated but its navy was for the first time halted. However, it was the first ever confrontation at sea to take place with the enemy ships placed hundreds of miles apart.

The firepower was carried to the opposition entirely by the planes stationed on the mighty carriers

ranged against each other, capable of causing wholesale devastation.

Meanwhile, the Battle of Midway proved to be a turning point in the fortunes of war and gave America the opportunity once more to assert naval superiority.

By May, Japan had control of New Britain, parts of Papua New Guinea and the majority of the Solomon Islands. It formed the outer edge of a Pacific empire which was fanning out towards Australia. The country's remaining aim was to secure the line of defence by conquering the remainder of Papua New Guinea.

The island of Midway was a glaring hole in Japan's line of defence

Japanese priorities changed, however, with the most effective nuisance raid mounted by the Americans to date. It came with Lieutenant Colonel J. Doolittle's bombing raid over Tokyo in April mounted through an open door from Midway. The island of Midway was held by a small garrison of American marines and was a glaring hole in Japan's line of defence. Although the damage caused during the 16-plane raid was light, it gave the Japanese hierarchy a shake up and compelled them to look again at domestic security.

EYE WITNESS

Normand N. Silver, from Montreal, was a stoker first class. A member of the Royal Canadian Navy Volunteer Reserve, he served aboard aircraft carriers HMS *Thames* and HMCS *Punchuard* and also the minesweeper HMCS *Quatisino*.

"I volunteered principally because I reckoned it was my duty. But we all guessed that if Hitler wasn't stopped then in 1945 or 1950 he'd maybe be sending his armies across to Canada.

The main action I saw was around the coast of Alaska in *Quatisino*. The Americans had a lot of their ships berthed up there and they didn't want another Pearl Harbor on their hands. So our job was to seek and destroy any Japanese subs that wanted to try their luck. It meant we were on round the clock patrol.

We were credited with killing one sub, but you could never know for sure. In the engine room you didn't get to see much anyway.

It's hard to explain the pressure you are under when you're fighting submarines. If you are a nervous person then you are in real trouble. You have to expect an attack every minute of every hour of every day. You don't know where the attack will come from and you don't know how long it will be before the next. You don't sleep much and you don't relax. I think that is the story of most men's war."

FIRST BLOOD

Admiral Yamamoto, confident in the continuing might of his navy, was appalled at the Tokyo air raid. He felt sure the best way ahead was to knock the heart out of the American navy once again. To do it he wanted to put Midway Island under threat.

Yamamoto knew America valued the island because of its proximity to Pearl Harbor and would defend it in force with its navy, so he planned to lure the remaining big ships into action and then destroy them.

Below: **The last gasp of the Japanese carrier *Shoho* before it sinks.**

Above: **USS *Lexington* sustains critical damage at the Battle of the Coral Sea.**

Meanwhile, the Japanese navy would also support a new thrust into Papua New Guinea where vital new forward bases could be installed.

Intelligence experts quickly grasped details of the preparations which would lead to the attack on Port Moresby, Papua New Guinea, after decoding Japanese communications. Tempted by the presence of some of Japan's finest ships, America's Admiral Chester Nimitz hastily drew together as many ships as he could for a surprise rendezvous with the Japanese in the Coral Sea.

Australian cruisers which had gone ahead to secure a vital seaway for the heavier ships came under attack from Japanese planes but miraculously escaped damage. So first blood in the four day battle went to the Americans when a wave of planes located the light carrier Shoho and blasted it out of the water. It left the Japanese in a quandary as they had no idea where the attacking aircraft had come from.

***The US tally included three direct hits on the aircraft carrier* Shokaku**

As night fell, Japanese planes were launched to locate their hidden enemy but, hampered by low cloud, were forced to ditch their bombs and head back to base. En route, they happened across the USS Yorktown which sent up aircraft for a confrontation. In total 17 Japanese planes were lost that night against only three American casualties. In fact, for a while both sides suffered from the main disadvantage that this new, long-distance warfare offered. Neither could locate the enemy ships.

TACTICAL VICTORY

The next day both sides sent waves of aircraft in pursuit of the other. The US tally included three direct hits on the aircraft carrier Shokaku which was forced to limp back to its home port for major repairs.

Meanwhile, the Japanese struck the carriers Yorktown and

Lexington. The Yorktown escaped with comparatively minor damage while the Lexington was crippled by three bombs and two torpedoes. It was to sink days later following an internal explosion. Both admirals decided against continuing the battle

The Lexington was to sink days later following an internal explosion

and pulled away from their respective battle lines.

Japan appeared to have inflicted the most damage on the opposition. In reality, however, the tactical victory belonged to the Americans. The Japanese had been contained and were forced to call off their strike at Port Moresby due to the large losses of essential aircraft.

◆ EYE WITNESS ◆

Mitsuo Fuchida, who led the air strike against Pearl Harbor, was aboard the aircraft carrier *Akagi* during the Battle of Midway.

"For Japan, the Battle of Midway was indeed a tragic defeat. The Japanese Combined Fleet, placing its faith in "quality rather than quantity" had long trained and prepared to defeat a numerically superior enemy. Yet at Midway a stronger Japanese force went down to defeat before a weaker enemy.

Not only were our participating surface forces far superior in number to those of the enemy but the initiative was in our hands. Nor were we inferior qualitatively in the crucial element of air strength which played a major role throughout the Pacific War. In spite of this we suffered a decisive defeat such as the modern Japanese navy had never before experienced or even dreamed possible.

With Midway as the turning point, the fortunes of war appeared definitely to shift from our own to the Allied side. The defeat taught us many lessons and impelled our navy, for the first time since the outbreak of war, to indulge in critical self examination.

The Japanese public, of course, was not told the truth about the battle. Instead, Imperial General Headquarters announcements tried to make it appear that both sides had suffered equal losses. The United States, however, promptly announced to the whole world the damaged inflicted on the Japanese acccurately naming the ships damaged and sunk. Thus it was clear that our efforts to conceal the truth were aimed at maintaining morale at home rather than keeping valuable knowledge from the enemy.

I myself had a rather painful taste of the extreme measures taken to preseve secrecy. During the battle I had been wounded on board *Akagi* and then transferred to hospital ship *Hikawa Maru* which brought me to Yokosuka Naval Base. I was not moved ashore until after dark when the streets of the base were deserted. Then I was taken to the hospital on a covered stretcher and carried in through the rear entrance. My room was placed in complete isolation. No nurses or corpsmen were allowed entry and I could not communicate with the outside.

In such a manner were those wounded at Midway cut off from the rest of the world. It was really confinement in the guise of medical treatment and I sometimes had the feeling of being a prisoner of war."

Above: Shokaku **pulled back to Japan following the Coral Sea battle.**

The Japanese High Command decided to abandon that first objective in favour of the capture of Midway, a far more ambitious undertaking. While the commanders had sought outright victory in the Coral Sea, they were convinced by their own glowing track record that the US navy could still be annhilated.

Once again intelligence reports gave the United States fair warning of the Japanese plans which they had tagged Operation MI. And again Admiral Nimitz called in as much support as he could from ships and submarines in the region. Aircraft carriers Enterprise and Hornet were summoned along with the damaged Yorktown which had been hurriedly repaired so it could rejoin the action.

Japanese commanders were convinced that the US Navy could be annihilated

They sailed with six cruisers, 14 destroyers and 19 submarines to the north of Midway to await the attackers. On the island itself the garrison had been strengthened and increased numbers of aircraft brought in.

The Japanese strike force, including half the navy's aircraft carriers, came from several directions, one arm to land troops, another to tackle the American naval presence.

At dawn on 4 June, bombers took off from Japanese aircraft carriers and blasted the land-based defenders of Midway. Aircraft from the island attempting to deflect the invaders suffered huge losses and made little impact. It seemed the Japanese navy was to escape once more intact.

SURPRISE RAID

But before a second wave of bombers could be launched, Japan's Vice-Admiral Chuichi Nagumo was told of the presence of enemy ships signalled by the first attack by their planes. Instead of the continuing bombardment of the already shattered small island, he decided to swing north and pursue the US Navy prey.

By now torpedo bombers from all the aircraft carriers had been launched and began a comprehensive strike lasting 55 minutes on three of Japan's aircraft carriers. Japanese pilots supported by anti-aircraft fire defended the ships fiercely. Of the 41 US planes which set out on that mission, only six returned. It seemed victory was in the grasp of the Japanese. Yet they barely had time to congratulate themselves on their luck and judgement when the subsequent wave of dive-bombers sent by the Americans arrived on the scene.

Of the 41 US planes which set out on that mission, only six returned

As the Japanese sailors and airmen struggled to rearm in the disarray,

Above: Akagi, **another Japanese navy gem, weaves its way out of fire at Midway.**

bombs rained down on them and exploded on the decks crowded with aircraft. Afterwards, Japanese sailors told how the raid took them by surprise – which is why the prized planes were crowded on deck. It took a matter of minutes to reduce the carriers to smoking crates. Two of the Japanese carriers, the Kaga and Soryu, sank within hours. The Akagi drifted hopelessly and helplessly until a Japanese submarine punctured it for the last time the following day.

It took a matter of minutes to reduce the carriers to smoking crates

Half an hour afterwards, bombers from an unscarred Japanese carrier, the Hiryu, went looking for revenge. Their target was the Yorktown on which the battle commander Rear-Admiral Frank Fletcher was based. A volley of hits during two onslaughts finally put paid to the veteran carrier which was abandoned by its crew later the same day. A Japanese submarine sent its skeleton to the bottom two days later.

It was not the end of the bloody battle, however. At 5pm, less than 12 hours after the conflict began, USS Enterprise – nicknamed the 'Big E' – launched bombers in pursuit of the Hiryu. They caught up with their target and sparked a catastrophic blaze on board. The Hiryu, Japan's fourth and final aircraft carrier in the offensive, was finally laid to rest by a Japanese cruiser.

Admiral Yamamoto continued his assault on Midway from the heavy cruisers that remained. But when two of them collided trying to evade an American submarine, he was finally convinced of its folly.

The American navy's Rear-Admiral Raymond Spruance risked one final foray against the Japanese, holing one of the already damaged cruisers and sinking the other. Even then Admiral Yamamoto was ready to spring a trap on the American fleet by luring them into combat with a light force and then pounce with much bigger guns.

HUGE VICTORY

Admiral Spruance was not to be drawn. Content with his enormous victory, he headed for home, leaving Yamamoto helpless in his wake. A Japanese submarine managed to claim one destroyer before Spruance pulled out of the region.

The decisive result was trumpeted around the Allied world. From Pearl

Below: **US giant USS *Yorktown* lists helplessly following Midway.**

Left: Admiral Raymond Spruance, an engineer of the Midway victory.

Harbor Admiral Nimitz announced: '. . . the enemy's damage is very heavy indeed, involving several ships in each of the carrier, battleship, cruiser and transport classes. This damage is far out of proportion to that which we have received.

'The brunt of the defence to date has fallen upon our aviation personnel, in which the Army, Navy and Marine Corps are all represented. They have added another shining page to their record of achievements.'

From a position of seemingly indomitable strength, the Japanese navy had within a few short days been for the first time mauled and gored. The defeat was so terrible that it was cloaked in secrecy in Japan for the duration of the war. While scores of heroic American pilots lost their lives in the battle, they inflicted devastation on their hitherto unbroken enemy and it was their courage alone that turned the tables. Four aircraft carriers, together with more than 300 aircraft and the cream of the Japanese naval pilots were at the bottom of the ocean. The steamroller successes of the Japanese forces had been stopped, Midway was saved and further plans by the Japanese to occupy other Pacific islands were shelved.

The steamroller successes of the Japanese forces had been stopped

EYE WITNESS

Dennis Bell, of Waterlooville, Hampshire, was one of the youngest seamen to sail with the D-Day invasion fleet. At 16 he was a galley boy in the merchant navy, serving aboard the converted troop ship *Liberation of Europe*.

'My clearest memory of the whole war was on VE day when our convoy was in mid-Atlantic. The sea was just like glass and suddenly these ten U-boats just rose out of the sea to surrender to us. It was a truly amazing sight.'

Below: Admiral Nimitz considers his next move from the bridge of a destroyer.

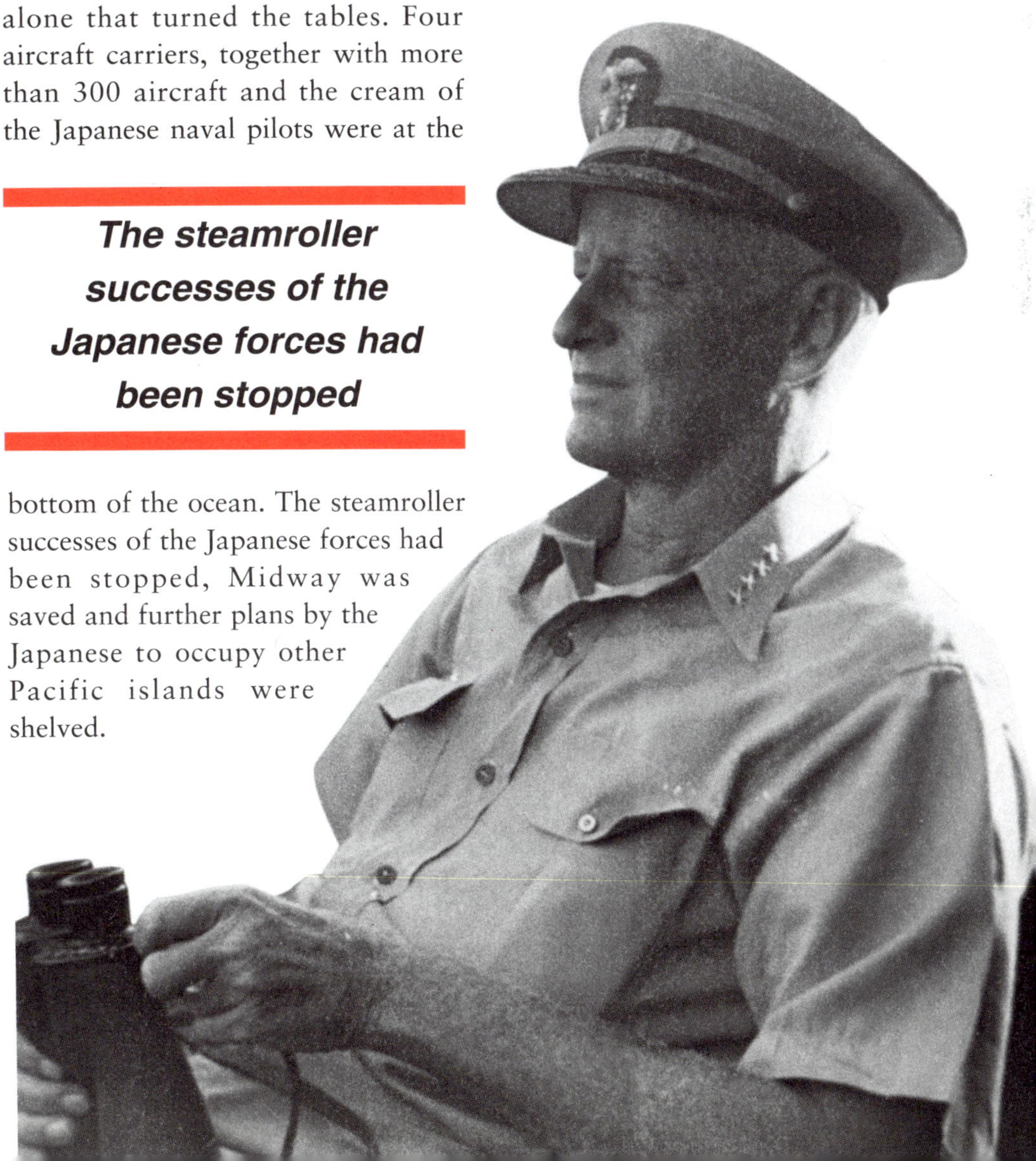

THE SOLOMONS

The Battle of Midway sent Admiral Yamamoto and his mariners home with a bloody nose. Yet the Japanese still fostered some aggressive ambitions, among them a plan to sink the remainder of the US Navy and once again win dominance over the Pacific.

By May 1942 Japanese forces occupied Tulagi, one of the Solomon Islands. The Americans were keen to keep this Pacific route open as it represented a vital line of communication with Australia. So American military planners devised a plan, 'Operation Watchtower', to rout the Japanese from the region.

Initially, US and Australian troops were to liberate Tulagi and a few other selected islands. Then their aim was to free the rest of the occupied Solomon Islands and Papua in New Guinea. The final phase of the operation would be the capture of the Bismarck Archipelago; New Britain and New Ireland.

The Americans busied themselves gathering their forces, including three aircraft carriers, a battleship, 14 cruisers and plenty of destroyers. After setting off from Wellington, New Zealand, on 22 July, there were four days of practice runs on a remote Pacific Island before the operation got underway.

Meanwhile, the Japanese were also making plans. They still harboured hopes of capturing Port Moresby in Papua, their target before the Battle of the Coral Sea. Instead of using a waterborne force this time, they would go overland. A fleet comprising five heavy and three light cruisers, five submarines and a number of destroyers was based at Rabaul on New Britain and the Japanese further tried

Above: **A Marine's eye-view of a Pacific landing operation, this one at Tulagi.**
Left: **A Grumann Hellcat fighter returns to USS *Lexington* in the Pacific.**
Below: **US Marines practise for their invasion of the Solomon Islands.**

to strengthen their position by building new airfields right across the occupied territories.

The islands they were fighting over offered little more than strategic value to either side. The Solomon Islands, discovered in the 16th century by the Spanish, had been a British Protectorate although two of

On 7 August, 11,000 US Marines landed on the Solomons without meeting opposition

the major islands fell under the domain of Australia. They stretch for some 600 miles in two roughly parallel lines encircling a waterway called The Slot.

It was a fighting man's nightmare. The climate was damp and humid encouraging thick jungle and forest to cling to the sides of the mountains which cropped up throughout the centres of the isles alongside smokey volcanoes. On the coastal plains there were, apart from coconut plantations, acres of dense, spikey grass, sharp as a knife.

On the morning of 7 August, 11,000 US Marines landed on Guadalcanal in the Solomons without meeting any opposition. Within 24 hours they had taken the airstrip as their own.

The three battalions that landed on Tulagi were not so lucky. The Marines encountered fierce resistance from the 1,500 Japanese defenders of the island. It cost the Marines 108 of their men before the island was theirs, in addition to many more wounded.

JAPAN ENRAGED

It was the work of a few days to win the islands. Ahead lay a bloody six months as they battled to keep them out of the hands of the Japanese.

The Japanese were surprised and enraged when they found out that one of their new prizes had been overrun. First response by Imperial General Headquarters was to send a convoy of

EYE WITNESS

Despite being sunk while a soldier in North Africa, Australian George Miles went on to join the US Army Small Ships Section.

I received a medical discharge from the Australian Army in 1943 but at the time nothing much appealed in civilian life in Sydney. Within six months I joined the US Army Water Transport Division and served in a couple of invasions in Indonesia, New Guinea and the Philippines.

With the amount of casualties suffered by the US merchant navy, they were prepared to make you a seaman in a matter of weeks. The first ship I signed on was all American. These men had never met an Australian before. They called me 'Limey' and reckoned I came from London. But there were a few Aussies in the force.

For the invasion at Leyte I was on a tug patrol. The amount of sea power the Americans had was incredible. There was no way they were going to lose.

Below: **The first wave of Marines find their feet on the Solomons.**

Left: **An enemy stronghold on the Solomons is blasted by US planes.**

500 troops to reinforce the islands. However, a US submarine put paid to the plan with a single torpedo. Those troops that survived were forced to turn back to New Britain.

However, their next strike was markedly more successful. Armed with reconnaissance information about the size and strength of the enemy forces, Admiral Mikawa and a rogue squadron slipped in to The Slot unnoticed by the watching Allied ships on 8 August, their silhouettes blotted out by bad weather.

SAVO ISLAND

Aided by flares dropped from his carrier planes, Admiral Mikawa gleefully caught sight of the Royal Australian Navy cruiser *Canberra* and the US Navy cruiser *Chicago*, patrolling The Slot. Both Allied ships were unaware their lines had been penetrated by enemy vessels. It meant the Japanese squadron was able to open up at point-blank range with shells and torpedoes.

Canberra came off worse. The damage that the ship sustained was so bad it had to be abandoned. *Chicago* escaped with just one hit from a torpedo. But before its gunners could fire back, the Japanese squadron was heading north, straight towards another Allied patrol. Three more American cruisers were set alight and sank. The Japanese squadron pulled out at speed, completely unscathed. Even though they had left the transports delivering to Guadalcanal untouched, victory in the Battle of Savo Island was theirs for the cost of 38 men, while more than 1,000 American and Australian sailors perished.

Eleven days later the action was once again at sea when a sizeable force of Japanese soldiers charged with winning back Guadalcanal set off from Rabaul under the protection of two aircraft carriers, a light carrier, two battleships, five cruisers and 17 destroyers.

Allied ships were unaware their lines had been penetrated by enemy vessels

Ready to meet them this time was an Allied task force of three aircraft carriers and a battleship. Japan's Admiral Kondo sent his light aircraft carrier ahead as a decoy. It drew the fire of the American fleet air arm and sank on the afternoon of 24 August. Meanwhile the larger carriers had also been spotted.

Right: **Japanese air power prior to the 'Marianas Turkey Shoot'.**

Right: **A kamikaze plane crashes into the sea short of its target.**

When the expected wave of Japanese aircraft arrived, there was a reception committee of US fighters to meet them, ably supported by anti-aircraft fire. Although the Japanese lost a number of planes, the Battle of the Eastern Solomons, as it was christened, was inconclusive. Both navies withdrew that night. It was the land-based bombers who later attacked the Japanese transports that forced them away from their destination.

The sorties were nicknamed the 'Tokyo Express' by the watching Marines

Afterwards, the Japanese navy ships boldly sped down The Slot with regularity, both to fire on the American positions and to land troops and supplies. Soon the sorties were nicknamed the 'Tokyo Express' by the watching Marines.

At the end of August the US aircraft carrier Saratoga was torpedoed by a submarine and was forced back to Pearl Harbor for repairs. The US naval strength in the area, already inferior to Japan's, continued to take a battering from both submarines and aircraft attacks.

America had to wait some six weeks before replying in kind. A squadron escorting some American transporters happened on a Japanese naval force which was preparing to fire on a US-controlled airstrip. In the confrontation that followed one Japanese cruiser and two destroyers were sunk for the cost of one American destroyer.

A major Japanese effort to recapture Guadalcanal was knocked back at the end of October but the Japanese navy was still not ready to lie down. At the ensuing Battle of Santa Cruz, the outnumbered Americans lost seventy aircraft compared to an estimated 100 downed from the Japanese ranks. The US carrier Enterprise was damaged, along with a battleship and a cruiser. All the Japanese ships stayed afloat although five sustained damage.

SAVAGE ACTION

It wasn't until the three-day naval battle of Guadalcanal that the American Navy found the outright victory which had eluded it so far. It began with a savage encounter between a small American escort force against a powerful Japanese squadron. Although the US contingent was cut through during the battle, which lasted just 24 minutes, it saved the Guadalcanal airstrip from bombardment and it bought valuable time for the pursuing US task force.

Two days afterwards, the Americans unleashed their firepower at the Japanese with another close range bloody battle at sea. A Japanese battleship was so badly damaged she had to be scuttled. One Japanese and three American destroyers were sunk. The key to the American success was the attack the next day on the transports bringing an attacking Japanese force to Guadalcanal. Three-fifths of the landing troops were annihilated.

Left: **Japanese ships scatter as US planes open fire from above.**

The rest were rendered an ineffective fighting force, trapped as they were without supplies or food.

The final conflict in seas surrounding the Solomons was the Battle of Tassaronga, which turned out to be equally damaging to both Japan and America. The losses suffered by the Japanese navy were sufficient to persuade its leaders not to venture again into such fateful waters.

Japanese destroyers went to the Solomons just once more, to help in the evacuation of troops from Guadalcanal in January 1943.

With every month that passed the Americans managed to reinforce their navy and its vital fleet air arm. There was little the Japanese could do to replace its lost ships, planes or pilots.

The Japanese Navy took its next severe pounding in port at Rabaul in October 1943. Aircraft from the growing number of American carriers in the region launched two raids. The tally of damage to the Japanese was a destroyer which sank and damage to seven cruisers and three more destroyers. In subsequent air battles an estimated two-thirds of the Japanese carrier aircraft were gunned down, the cream of its pilots lost forever. It finally squeezed the Japanese navy out of Rabaul once and for all.

US SUPERIORITY

At home Japan tried to nurture a new generation of navy pilots to replace those it had lost in the Solomons and soon afterwards. Their destination was the Marianas, a series of islands being heavily reinforced by the Japanese to fend off US invasion.

But the students were ill-equipped to deal with intense warfare and they were lost in their droves. In the two-day Battle of the Philippine Sea in June 1944 the Japanese navy received yet another drubbing from Task Force 58 commanded by Admiral Spruance. At last the Americans had found an antidote to Japan's Zero fighter. The new US Hellcat was faster and more powerful.

It was known among Americans as 'The Great Marianas Turkey Shoot' after wave upon wave of Japanese planes were bagged and brought down. In total the Japanese lost 223 aircraft. Only 17 aircraft returned from an attacking force of 69 in the first wave of aircraft. In the next wave the Japanese lost 98 out of its force of 130 planes and, although a third wave returned intact having failed to find its target, in the disastrous fourth wave just nine survived out of 82. The Americans were down by just 29 aircraft. In addition, three Japanese aircraft carriers were sunk.

Afterwards the Americans had undisputed superiority at sea in the Pacific. They outnumbered the Japanese in all classes of ship, boasting 17 battleships to Japan's nine, 12 fleet carriers compared to four, 47 escort carriers against three and 155 submarines up against just 48. None of the four Japanese aircraft carriers had planes aboard and all were listing from battle damage.

EYE WITNESS

Swedish-born Nels Olson, 72, from Chicago, USA, was a gunner in the US Navy Armed Guard, who later served in the Pacific at the time of the Japanese surrender.

'My war ended in the Pacific. I arrived on the island of Okinawa two or three weeks after the Japanese surrender. All the guys wore guns when they went ashore but there were no problems. The Japanese bowed to us whenever they saw us. It was like they went out of their way to show they did not want to fight.

For a country that caused us such problems I was amazed at how primitive some of the people were. I once had to supervise the unloading of coal from a cargo ship. They did it by sending men on board with two buckets strapped to their shoulders. It was amazing to watch.'

AMPHIBIOUS WARFARE

When British, Australian and New Zealand troops tried to land at Gallipoli during World War I, the sea ran red with their blood.

Bullets from defending Turkish guns rained down on unfortunate troops as soon as they emerged from boats just short of the shore line. It remains one of the most appalling military disasters in history in which there were more than a quarter of a million casualties on the Allied side alone.

Winston Churchill, then First Lord of the Admiralty and a keen exponent of the plan, resigned over the Gallipoli debacle and it blighted his career for years afterwards.

Though the adventure achieved little, it served to illustrate the glaring gap in military manoeuvres which reduced soldiers trying to take a fortified coast to cannon fodder.

Left: **The Americans led the field in the development of amphibious techniques.** *Below:* **LVTs and LCVPs approach the island of Aguni Shima in the Pacific.**

The lesson was not lost on Major Earl Ellis in the United States. He realised the importance of safe transport of troops from ship to shore during invasion. His aim was to give American Marines the best chance of survival. As early as 1921 he had written a 50,000-word plan which was intended as a blueprint for a Marine advance in the Pacific. He argued that men should be specifically trained to overcome the hazards of amphibious warfare and that the Marines were the best task force to undergo that instruction.

LANDING VEHICLES

Ellis wrote: 'It is not enough that the troops be skilled infantry men and jungle men or artillery men of high morale. They must be skilled water men and jungle men who know it can be done – marines with marine training.'

By 1933 the Fleet Marine Force came into being to oversee the challenge of amphibious landings. There followed a series of experiments with tracked landing vehicles able to travel in the sea, offering protection to soldiers on leaving landing boats. It wasn't until the war years, however, that an effective ship-to-shore craft was constructed, the

It wasn't until the war that an effective ship-to-shore craft was constructed

LVT or Landing Vehicle, Tracked. Even then, due to its mechanical shortcomings, the 'amtrac' was mainly used to travel up beaches rather than on to them.

Boatbuilder Andrew Higgins, from New Orleans, then came to the notice of the US Marines after he built a shallow-draft vessel for crossing the Mississippi River. It beached with ease and could be pulled back into the water at speed. Here was a

craft far superior to anything else the marines had found.

Bizarrely, the US Navy's Bureau of Ships was reluctant to adopt a design from someone outside the service. Continuing its costly probes into making landing craft for years afterwards, it still failed to come up with an adequate rival to Higgins' model. The fiasco was roundly condemned by a Senate Committee during the war.

That original Higgins design finally became the father of the LCP(L)s, Landing Craft Personnel (Large) used by both Britain and the Americans during World War II. Work continued throughout the war to perfect landing craft of various capabilities; some were armed, some were ocean-going; some were tracked. They proved a formidable amphibious force.

MARINE TRAINING

The Japanese were also investigating the possibilities of amphibious landing craft. The Japanese army built an early version of LSDs (Landing Ships, Dock) for their operations in China during the 1930s called Shinshu Maru. Inside its cavernous interior the vessel could house a number of landing craft which rolled up a ramp and out of the ship's open doors.

In order to land troops, they had a 46ft landing craft which they modified to bear arms for the men of the Special Naval Landing Force, the equivalent of the marines.

In Britain, only fleeting interest was expressed in the dilemma. Recovering from its battering in World War I, the service chiefs in the main neglected to look ahead and plan for another war. It wasn't until 1937 that Admiral Sir Reginald Ernest-Ernle-Plunkett-Drax suggested that several brigades of Royal Marines should be trained especially for amphibious landings. The eventual outcome was the establishment of the Inter-Service Training

In Britain, service chiefs neglected to look ahead and plan for another war

◆ EYE WITNESS ◆

Gordon Kendall, from Portsmouth, UK, served with 4 Commando.

"British commandos were assigned to set out guns on either side of the Dieppe basin ready for a sea-borne Canadian invasion force. Around 150 of us went ashore before dawn, did the job and got out.

The Canadians didn't arrive until much later. That was a mistake because they were absolutely chopped to pieces. We reckoned that of the 3,000 who went ashore, 900 died on the beach and more than a thousand were taken prisoner.

The irony is that they should never even have been there. The British Northumberland Division had been training for this operation but the Canadians were restless and took it over. It seems some of their commanding officers were hungry for action after hanging around in the UK for so long."

Below: **US troops emerge from the bowels of USS *LSM-168* in March 1945.**

Above: **An armada of LSTs offload onto a recently captured beach.**

and Development Centre near Portsmouth, in southern England, which involved all the defence forces and developed a policy for amphibious operations which remained key for the duration of the war.

At last staff in the unit addressed the problems of specialised landing craft, navy gunfire support, floating piers to aid the disembarkation of tanks and trucks and an array of workable tactics.

TANK SHIPMENT

The ranks of the Royal Marines, standing at just 12,000 when war broke out, were substantially boosted. Their role of manning guns aboard Royal Navy ships and guarding navy shore-based establishments was expanded to man commando raiding parties.

Following the evacuation of British troops from Dunkirk in 1940, the need for armoured ocean-going craft able to carry men and machines into shallow water was once again highlighted. While there was relief at the number of soldiers who got out of France in one piece, they barely managed to bring back a gun between them. The army lost every tank and major piece of artillery it had committed to France at the outbreak of war. If a suitable transport craft had been available, at least some of it might have been saved.

Now Churchill's mind was concentrated on the issue. Until his men and tanks could be safely transported across the Channel, there would be no opportunity for Churchill to make up the ground he had lost in France. Tanks were a primary tool of war and shipment of them in any amphibious assault was vital.

A British prototype Landing Ship, Tank (LST) came into being in October 1940. It was further improved when tankers made in Britain especially to traverse a troublesome sand bank in South America were converted to carry tanks. These were fitted to carry 20 tanks or 33 trucks but were unable to come close into shore.

A new design was thought up to overcome the problem. The difficulties posed in getting the ships produced in Britain's hard-pressed shipyards was overcome when America agreed to take on the contract. Shipyards across the States became involved in producing LSTs, launching the first of the new design on 7 September 1942. Before the war was over, 1,050 more came out of US yards to see action in amphibious landings across the world. They would join the Landing Ships,

The army lost every single tank and major piece of artillery it had committed to France

Right: **Motorised equipment from an LST rolls on to a 'rhino' to reach the sand.**

Infantry (LSI) and Landing Ships, Dock (LSD) already in service. But although the seeds of a successful amphibious landing force had been sown, there was a long way to go before it would threaten the Reich.

DIEPPE LANDINGS

As if to emphasise the point, the Allied landings in Dieppe in August 1942 ended in almost complete disaster. The Allies referred to it as a raid while Hitler insisted it was a fully-fledged invasion.

The Allied force consisted of 5,000 Canadians, 1,057 British, 50 Americans and a few Free French soldiers. Setting out under the cover of early morning darkness, they ran into difficulty when the landing craft which took them from their ships to the shore were swept along the beach. Armed German trawlers happened on the scene and began shooting at one of the British sections.

Now the Germans were fully alerted and greeted the arrival of 27 light tanks with a hail of gunfire. All were destroyed while the landing forces suffered appalling casualties. It was just 9am when the troops were pulled out. More than 1,500 prisoners were taken and most of the equipment was left scattered on the beach.

The Germans greeted the arrival of 27 light tanks with a hail of gunfire

A clutch of Allied boats was sunk and almost 100 of the aircraft dispatched to provide aerial cover were shot down. It was the largest in a succession of raids which met with varying degrees of success.

The Dieppe incident led Prime Minister Churchill and other British commanders to doubt the wisdom of making another attempt against well-fortified German positions, despite American pressure to open a second front in Europe.

However, some valuable lessons were learned from the raids in time to execute the biggest amphibious landing ever, on D-Day.

◆ EYE WITNESS ◆

Henry 'Marty' Martin, from Chicopee, Massachusetts, USA, stormed Omaha beach in a DD (Duplex Drive amphibious tank). He landed in the first wave aboard LCT 586.

"My job was to drop the ramp. These men trained to get out in 30 seconds but we didn't have time to check that they all got out safely. We did four drops that day.

For our first we laid off 200 yards because it was so rough. The next one, though, we went right on to the beach. We were carrying three tanks and they had to get in close.

I watched the first tank take off to the right. He made it, but the second took a direct hit as he tried to follow. The third stayed closer to the shore and looked to be OK.

As they left a US officer came up to me literally holding the insides of his stomach in his hands. He was one of the underwater demolition experts who had gone in in advance of the landings. Those guys didn't have very good luck. I think nine in every ten were killed.

He told me we were the first ship to come right on to the beach. We got him back to the hospital ship but I never knew how he made out.

Sometimes historical accounts fail to mention the disputes and the arguments that took place. There was one officer who had it in for me. After D-Day I got a ten-day leave to Kilmarnock in Scotland and the thought of going back to work for this guy meant I decided to unofficially extend that leave for another ten days.

I served 30 days in the brig at Plymouth for that. But I reckoned that just because a man's an officer doesn't mean he can't be an asshole as well!"

Below: **A few moment's relaxation by an empty landing craft for weary troops.**

◆ EYE WITNESS ◆

Ernie Marshall joined the Royal Navy at the end of 1942 aged 18. After three months training he joined a combined operations unit and was stationed on *LCT 554*.

‘When I saw it my heart dropped. It looked pretty rough. The living quarters and the engine room were at the back while the tanks were in the front. There were 12 of us aboard. I was a stoker in the engine room. I just learnt as I went, I had no training whatsoever. Eventually we sailed to North Africa. It seemed like the whole of the Atlantic was coming up at us. Then we had to slide down these huge waves. I stayed in the engine room.

We worked every port up to Tripoli. Once we carried German prisoners of war.

Then we joined the landings at Sicily. We beached at 4am when it was very quiet. Next morning the Germans really came at us. We stayed there ferrying supplies for a couple of months until we went up to Anzio. We were stuck there for three months surrounded by Germans. The beachhead was about five miles inland. Once the Germans broke through and got to within two miles of the beach. Eventually, they were pushed back again.

The long range guns were more frightening than anything. Shells just landed without warning. One morning a plane attacked us. Shrapnel from one of its bombs came right through the stern, across the mess deck, through the next steel bulk head and into the engine room. Everywhere was filled with smoke and sparks. One bloke had an injured shoulder but the rest of us survived.

That afternoon we were alongside a boat unloading supplies when a bomb from a plane went straight into the hold. We managed to get ashore. Survivors got thrown into the water and were shouting to us for help. We fished a lot out of the water but we couldn't stop because the ship was burning so fiercely. That was the worst day of the war for me.

It was two and a half years before I got home. On the whole I enjoyed the experience. The rest of the crew became like family. The captain never gave us any trouble and we had some good times. I had never travelled before so to see Arabs in their African villages was really something.’

For example, specially trained civilian aircraft recognition teams from the Royal Observer Corps put to sea with the troops on 6 June 1944. This was to cut the rate of Allied aircraft shot down by jittery comrades on the ground.

At least the design of specialised landing craft was improved. They retained their speed and low silhouettes but were substantially enlarged to carry more men. Their armament they carried was also beefed up to provide greater support for the men they off-loaded.

The beaches of Normandy, unlike that of Dieppe, were away from major towns where German defences were strongest.

Yet still some avoidable mistakes were made. In the rough seas off the Normandy coast, British soldiers were instructed to carry not only their 20lb packs but also bicycles for use in France. On arrival, they were told to ditch the cycles in order to fight for their lives – and never saw the cumbersome two-wheelers that they had lugged on to the sands again.

No amount of improvements in the technique of amphibious landings could save the ‘poor, bloody infantry’ from being contained in cramped vessels for hours, sometimes days, on end before the final moment of invasion came. Often they suffered from sea-sickness. The food was generally poor and home comforts were lacking. Only the lucky ones got to sleep in hammocks.

Food was generally poor and home comforts were lacking

Before attacking Guam in July 1944, the US 3rd Marine Division spent weeks suffering like this at sea, most of them in dreadful weather conditions. The Channel weather in on D-Day was likewise awful.

Below: **Australian troops boarding a beach landing ship after successful operations at Lae, New Guinea.**

JAPAN'S LAST GASP

When America's war horse was harnessed, it galloped through the Pacific at a thundering pace. Advances made in 1944 by the combined efforts of the Army, Navy and Marine Corps mimicked those of the Japanese three years before.

By now the US strength at sea was awesome. Since the outbreak of the war with Japan a further 21 aircraft carriers had come into service capable of holding a total of about 3,000 planes.

That was in addition to a splendid array of new battleships, transports, cruisers, destroyers and landing craft newly arrived and ready for action.

On the other hand, the Japanese had suffered severe losses at sea and were continuing to do so. Apart from naval conflicts, the Japanese ships had to contend with the numerous American submarines now patrolling the Pacific in force.

Tiny Japan, so dependent on the resources it imported from overseas, was unable to replenish the fleet, with much of its merchant fleet being sunk bringing home vital war production materials. By 1944 two thirds of the tanker fleet bringing oil to Japan from the South Pacific fields had been wrecked by the Allies. While 40 per cent of the oil produced in those fields reached Japan in 1942, only 13.5 per cent was unloaded at Japanese ports in 1944 thanks to the efficiency of the submarines and fleet ships. Oil reserves were dwindling fast, threatening to grind the war effort to a halt. Hopelessly outnumbered, it seemed on paper that Japan's navy was all but finished.

When it became clear that the US was preparing to attack the Philippines in the autumn of 1944, however, Japan drew up the plans for one final sea battle which could have tipped the balance in its favour. It was a simple manoeuvre by what remained of the Japanese navy but might have been enough to defend

In the autumn of 1944 Japan drew up plans for one final sea battle

Left: **All eyes turn skywards when a Kamikaze aircraft is spotted in the vicinity.**
Below: **Vice Admiral Jisaburo Ozawa was defeated by superior US tactics.**
Bottom: **The scale of the US seapower is illustrated in this picture of Task Force 58 in the Pacific.**

Above: **Vice-Admiral William Halsey looks out to sea and draws up a winning strategy for the American fleet.**

the Philippines. And it was a gamble worth risking for the Japanese. If the Americans had installed themselves on the Philippines, it would have meant the end of oil supplies from

The arrival of Admiral Ozawa and his decoy carriers went unnoticed

the Dutch East Indies, now more crucial than ever before to the teetering Japanese.

After the war, Japan's Admiral S. Toyoda explained his country's actions: 'If the worst should happen there was a chance that we would lose the entire fleet; but I felt that chance had to be taken . . . should we lose in the Philippine operations, the shipping lane to the south would be completely cut off so that the fleet, if it should come back to Japanese waters, could not obtain its fuel supply. There would be no sense in saving the fleet at the expense of the the loss of the Philippines.'

In essence, Japan's ploy was to use what was left of the carrier fleet as a decoy to lure the main thrust of the American navy away from the Philippines. Once the large ships were out of the way, a two-pronged attack from the sea was planned on Leyte, the small island in the centre of the Philippines on which the Americans had already began an assault.

AMERICAN ATTACK

The operation began badly for the Japanese. One arm of the fleet earmarked to blast Leyte was itself fired on by American submarines on 23 October, well before it reached its destination. Three cruisers were badly damaged. There was a two-fold result to this action. The strength of this attacking arm was depleted and all the American shipping for miles around became focused on this single Japanese force. Despite frantic efforts to announce his presence by uncoded radio messages, the arrival of Admiral Ozawa and his decoy carriers went unnoticed by the Americans.

Now American battleships joined the attack on the hapless Japanese detachment whose brief had been to slip unobtrusively into the Philippine Sea. Japanese land-based bombers as

COUSINS

General Douglas MacArthur was an eighth cousin of Winston Churchill and a sixth cousin of Franklin Roosevelt. All three shared an ancestor in the shape of Sarah Barney Belcher of Taunton, Massachusetts.

well as those from the distant carriers rained bombs on the American fleet, crippling the carrier Princeton.

There was a high price for this success, however. The relentless onslaught by American fighter planes finally sank the majestic Musashi, one of the biggest battleships in the world. It had been hit by 19 torpedoes and 17 bombs. Japanese commander Admiral Kurita finally broke off from the action and appeared to retreat.

Above: **Devastation among Japanese shipping in the run-up to the invasion of the Philippine island of Leyte.**

BATTLE OF LEYTE

The absence of Japan's aircraft carriers was spotted by the sharp-witted Vice-Admiral William 'Bull' Halsey, who was in control of the American fleet. When he sent out reconnaissance planes to assess the movements of the Japanese fleet, Ozawa was finally detected. It seemed a golden opportunity to Halsey who gathered up his entire force to pursue the prized carriers, Japan's last surviving ship of the type in action.

Almost as soon as American backs were turned, Kurita reversed his course and began steaming towards his initial target once more, Leyte.

American sea defences were badly lacking after Halsey set off with his full complement of ships. Mostly it comprised a small force protecting the landing beaches at Leyte, just six escort carriers and five destroyers. In charge, Vice-Admiral T. C. Kinkaid sent a series of urgent messages to Halsey, asking him to return at once. Halsey, however, was determined to snare the carriers once and for all. He refused to turn around until he delivered some decisive damage to the carrier force. Only time would tell if his instincts were the right ones.

Japan's remaining battleships were no more than sitting ducks to the enemy

Meanwhile, the destroyers were defending the vulnerable section of the US fleet as best they could. One escort carrier and three destroyers were lost, however, in its retreat.

Now Kurita was steaming towards the Leyte Gulf where a collection of US transports and men lay wide open to attack. Then he hesitated. As Kinkaid watched and waited with bated breath, Kurita finally pulled his forces to the north, away from the beach targets.

Thanks to confusion among the intercepted radio messages aboard Kurita's ship, he believed Halsey and his powerful ships were only 70 miles away when in fact there were hundreds of miles between them. He was also gravely concerned about the risk of attack by air when he himself had no air cover.

Left: **The carrier USS *Princeton* is hosed after taking a direct hit from a bomber during the Battle of Leyte.**

SITTING DUCKS

While the survivors of Kurita's force escaped, the fate of the carriers gave credence to Halsey's actions. All four – Chitose, Zuikaku, Zuiho and Chiyoda – were sunk, completing the effective destruction of the Japanese navy. With the long-range power of aircraft, Japan's remaining battleships were no more than sitting ducks to the enemy. There was little

◆ EYE WITNESS ◆

Yasuo Kuwahara was a skilled Japanese pilot who was in a Kamikaze squadron in the final year of the war.

'It was New Year's Day 1945 at Hiro Air Base in western Honshu. Captain Yoshiro Tsubaki, commander of the Fourth Fighter Squadron, has just called a special meeting. A silence settled over us – only the patter of rain on the roof. The captain permitted us to sit while he stands, arms folded, eyes dark and unblinking – seemingly to spear us one by one.

After a long while, he spoke sonorously: "The time has at last arrived. We are faced with a great decision."

Again, he pauses but I feel it coming – the fear, greater than I have yet known. Death is there with us, enfolding each man, lingering, growing stronger. And the words from our captain flow so strangely.

"Any of you unwilling to give your lives as divine sons of the great Nippon empire will not be required to do so. Those incapable of accepting this honour will raise their hands – now."

Once more silence and death are almost palpable. The rain has subsided to a soft drizzle. Then hesitantly, timidly, a hand goes up, then another and another . . . six in all. The decision is mine; I can choose to live or die. Hasn't the captain just said so? But somehow... Of course, I want to live. But my hands – they remain at my sides trembling. I want to raise them but I can't. I want to raise my hands, even my soul would have me do it. Am I a coward? I cannot do it.

"Ah so," Captain Tsubaki fixes those who have responded in his stare. "It is good to know early exactly where we stand." They are summoned before us. "Here gentlemen," he points to the ashen faces, "are six men who have openly admitted their disloyalty. Since they are completely devoid of honour – without spirit – it becomes our duty to provide them with some. These men shall be Hiro's first attack group."

The breath, held so long within me, struggled out. I want to draw in more air, to expel it with relief, but something clenches inside. Six men from my squadron have just been picked for death. Hiro's first human bombs.'

Above: **A Japanese destroyer is smashed in two at Ormoc, Leyte, by a US B-25.**

more they could contribute to Japan's war effort.

From first to last, the three-day Battle of Leyte Gulf was the largest in history. In total, 282 ships were engaged along with hundreds of aircraft. It took the title of largest battlefrom the World War I Battle of Jutland when 250 British and German ships ships had met in combat, with only five seaplanes.

> ***Those who felt disgraced in some way would commit 'hari kiri'***

At the end of it, the Japanese had lost not only four carriers but also three battleships, six heavy cruisers, three light cruisers and eight destroyers. The triumph clearly belonged to the Americans whose casualties amounted to just one light carrier, two escort carriers and three destroyers.

Yet had the whim of the Japanese Admiral Kurita been different on the day and had he chosen to bombard the American beach positions, history might have had a different story to tell.

SUICIDE SQUADS

The Battle of Leyte Gulf is not only remembered as being the biggest naval battle ever. It was also the first to see the co-ordinated use of kamikazes – Japanese suicide squads.

Among the Japanese there was a strict code of honour. It had been instilled in them for centuries that death was better than dishonour or defeat. The first form of ritual suicide in Japan, called 'seppuku', was reserved by law for the samurai and was considered a privilege. Suicides could equally be carried out as a mark of respect.

Centuries later, those who felt disgraced in some way would commit 'hari kiri', literally translated to 'a cut to the stomach'. The aim for the person committing suicide was to disembowel themselves by using a ceremonial sword, an agonising process. As the years wore on, many made a symbolic cut in the stomach before turning a gun on themselves.

Surrender was abhorred by the Japanese, particularly among the troops, which explains the antipathy they displayed towards their own Japanese victim, the latter would devote his last burst of energy to pulling the pin from his final grenade, killing both men outright.

DESPERATE ACTS

Others would strap explosives to their bodies and hurl themselves at tanks or enemy positions to cause as much devastation as possible. Until now, these desperate acts were committed very much on an individual basis. But by 1944, staring into the jaws of defeat, the Japanese commanders decided to orchestrate suicide missions to cause the maximum hardship and loss of life to their enemies. Behind the enterprise

Japanese commanders orchestrated suicide missions to cause maximum loss of life

was Vice-Admiral Takijiro Onishi who himself committed hari kiri at the end of the war.

Kamikaze pilots in small planes would target the deck of an enemy ship. While bombs dropped by planes often fell short of the mark, the kamikazes' aim was unerringly accurate. British ships which generally boasted more deck armoury than

Above: USS _St Lô_ takes a direct hit from a kamikaze in the Battle of Leyte.
Right: USS _Suwanee_ gets running repairs after sustaining damage from a kamikaze.

prisoners of war. Many Japanese servicemen readily chose suicide rather than shame. High ranking officers also used to inspire courage and commitment among their men by killing themselves.

This made the Japanese particularly difficult enemies in the field. They were reluctant to be rescued if their missions went awry. In the sea, mystified Allied sailors watched in disbelief as the survivors of a wrecked ship tried to drown themselves or cut their own throats if they were armed. For if any unfortunate Allied soldier stopped to help a wounded or dying their American counterparts were better defended against such attacks.

There were also plans for suicide motorboats to target major ships. Beneath the waves there were one-man midget submarines which would set themselves on a collision course with a much larger vessel. These were difficult tactics to counter.

kamikaze squads whether the men were willing to die or not.

Inevitably, it undermined the success of the squads. Those without the necessary iron nerve were just as likely to plunge themselves and their aircraft into the sea instead of a ship, representing a waste of valuable resources. In a panic, many chose the first ships they saw to descend on. These were generally strategically less important than others in the fleet, once again wasting man and machine. Others would fly off in search of a specified target and return claiming the ship they were after could not be found. There were many accidents too, as the fuel-starved Japanese economised with all-important oil and stoked up the kamikaze aircraft with 50 per cent alcohol. If the aircraft engine failed, it was impossible to restart.

Commanders had no idea about the kamikaze success rate as there was no one left to report a result.

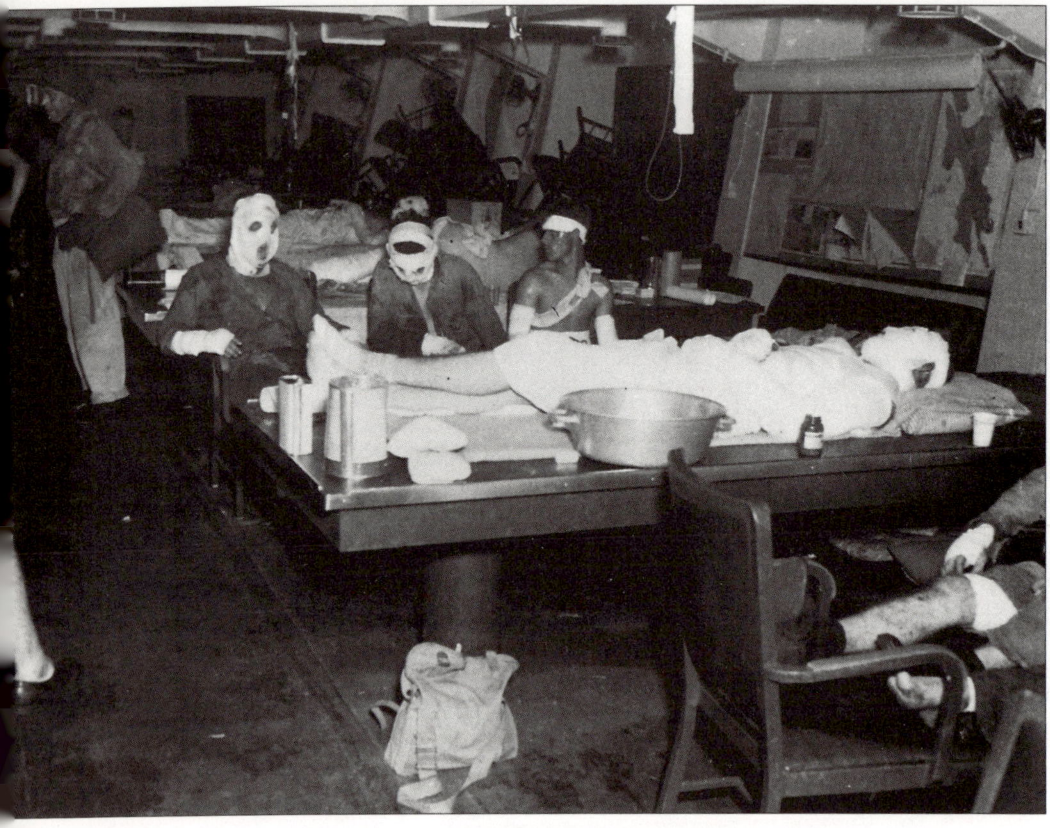

Above: **Wardroom of the carrier USS *Suwanee* becomes an emergency sick bay after the kamikaze attack during the Battle of Leyte Gulf.**

Stepping forward for these 'special' one-way missions were upright, traditional, fervent and deeply patriotic young men who thought little of laying down their lives for their country. They were, however, the elite. Despite the glory heaped on such pilots in domestic propaganda, the volunteers for the kamikaze ('divine wind') squads were drying up. Japanese commanders had no choice but to brand units as

After the war, Japan's Lieutenant-General Torashiro Kawabe explained the reasoning behind kamikaze attacks. 'We believed that our spiritual convictions and moral strength could balance your material and scientific advantages. We did not consider our attacks to be 'suicide'. The pilot did not start out on his mission with the intention of committing suicide. He looked upon himself as a human bomb which would destroy a certain part of the enemy fleet... he died happy in the conviction that his death was a step towards the final victory.'

Those without the necessary iron nerve were just as likely to plunge into the sea

At the Battle of Leyte Gulf, six aircraft took off from Cebu in the Philippines on 25 October 1944. Two hours later when they arrived at Leyte the planes deliberately rammed the US carriers Santee and Suwanee, causing extensive damage. The next day one American ship, St Lô, was sunk by use of kamikaze.

BEST DEFENCE

In the next three months, 22 Allied naval vessels were sunk by kamikaze pilots against 12 holed in conventional air attack. A further 110 kamikaze strikes damaged shipping.

They were a hazard which was to plague the Americans, Australians and British for the rest of the war. The best defence against kamikaze was interception by fighter planes or a volley of anti-aircraft fire, but it was not guaranteed to work. A lone Japanese pilot could still bring about the deaths of many.